Greece & Rome

NEW SURVEYS IN THE CLASSICS No. 32

THE INVENTION OF PROSE

BY

SIMON GOLDHILL

Published for the Classical Association

OXFORD UNIVERSITY PRESS

2002

OXFORD
UNIVERSITY PRESS

Great Clarendon Street, Oxford OX2 6DP

Oxford University Press is a department of the University of Oxford
and furthers the University's aim of excellence in research, scholarship,
and education by publishing worldwide in

Oxford New York

Athens Auckland Bangkok Bogotá Bombay Buenos Aires Calcutta
Cape Town Chennai Dar es Salaam Delhi Florence Hong Kong Istanbul
Karachi Kuala Lumpur Madrid Melbourne Mexico City Mumbai
Nairobi Paris São Paulo Singapore Taipei Tokyo Toronto Warsaw
with associated companies in Berlin Ibadan

Oxford is a registered trade mark of Oxford University Press
in the UK and in certain other countries

ISSN 0017–3835
ISBN 0–19–852523–0

Typeset by Joshua Associates Ltd., Oxford
Printed in Great Britain
on acid-free paper by
Bell and Bain Ltd., Glasgow

PREFACE

Greece & Rome Surveys are changing. They were inaugurated thirty-five years ago as brief essays to direct bright students and their teachers towards significant areas of critical concern in a major author's work and the relevant bibliography. Since then, they have moved on to more extended essays on areas of thought, as well as on particular authors. This essay is designed to introduce such a general area – namely, the world of fifth- and fourth-century Greek prose. There are already Surveys on historiography and on science and on 'ancient thought' (primarily philosophy). This book is not intended to reproduce or cannibalize those excellent studies. Rather, this Survey takes a different, complementary look at the cultural revolution of the classical *polis* through one of its new ways of writing. Central to this project is *rhetoric* as a science and a practice – but it has proved impossible to think about rhetoric seriously without looking at it across the differing developing prose genres. It is an essay designed first to put rhetoric in a nuanced context of writing; second – and perhaps most importantly – to recapture some of the novelty and excitement of a period when genres now so familiar to us were being established. This is not a book on 'prose style': the requirements of translation and transliteration forbid extensive analysis of such precisions of expression. Nor is this a full survey of the possible or even common discussions of all of the authors and genres mentioned: in the notes I have provided a spare and critical (rather than exhaustive) bibliography, focusing on works in English for what I assume will be a mainly Anglophone readership, and indicating where further work can be found. I have not indicated every debt, so as not to burden the text with an excessive apparatus, and the notes are solely for following up issues of interest for the reader. If this book turns some of its readers back towards Greek prose writing with a fresh eye – and a wish to read on, more deeply and with a new sense of the critical issues involved – then the project will have been a success.

My thanks are gratefully recorded to Robin Osborne for reading and commenting on the whole manuscript, and to Robert Wardy for reading Chapter IV.

Simon Goldhill

CONTENTS

I. INTRODUCTION

There's a famous moment in Molière's comedy *The Bourgeois Gentleman* when the philosopher rather pompously distinguishes between prose and verse; Jourdain, the old buffoon, comments with wonderment, 'I have been speaking prose for forty years and I never knew it!'. It is easy to take prose for granted. It's what everyone speaks, after all (and always has done); it's what is taught at school as the normal and expected manner of communication. Prose is inevitably thought to be the 'natural' way to write. So how could a book be called *The Invention of Prose*? Hasn't prose always been with us?

In this book, I am going to explore a quite different and less intuitively obvious claim. I want to suggest not merely that in the West prose as a written form flourishes for the first time in the fifth century BCE in Greece, but also that prose first takes the stage as a trendy, provocative, modern and highly intellectualized form of writing. Indeed, this new prose writing is integral to the cultural revolution we call the Greek enlightenment. Put most aggressively, the invention of prose is fundamental to the very foundation of Western culture.

This argument needs unpacking, more slowly, piece by piece. Let's begin by outlining the historical case. Here, I must start with a few words about archaic Greece – which is the name conventionally used for the period leading up to the explosive cultural events of the fifth century (classical Greece).[1] I have one simple point to make: in archaic Greece, what's *authoritative*, what *matters*, is performed and recorded *in verse*. It does not matter if you talk of politics, or of war or sexual adventures, religious celebration or the highest level of intellectual argument, the privileged medium of expression is poetry.

Consider for a moment the range of writing that has come down to us from this period – texts which have proved to be extremely influential throughout Greek culture and beyond, and which testify to the social turmoil and vibrant creative life of archaic society. The most important are undoubtedly the epics of Homer, the *Iliad* and the *Odyssey*, which

---

[1] On archaic Greece, the best starting point is Osborne (1996) with excellent bibliography; Snodgrass (1971) is an essential beginning on the archaeology and its importance, to be read with Morris (1987) and, from a cultic perspective, de Polignac (1995) (to be followed up with Alcock and Osborne (1994)). On cultural matters, a stimulating set of essays is Dougherty and Kurke (1993). Andrewes (1956) is still an excellent read on political matters. On cities other than Athens, see e.g. Cartledge (1979) and in general Finley (1981).

remain touchstones of value throughout the history of Greece – read, listened to, absorbed as signs of what it means to be Greek. In the *Iliad* and *Odyssey*, Greeks of all cities found a history of the past; stories of heroes whose genealogies stretch into the present; models of behaviour, patterns of thought, and forms of expression. It would be difficult to overemphasize the influence of these texts on the cultural life of Greece. They provide a set of images by which a Greek man continued to make sense of his world. It would be nigh on impossible to find an ancient Greek text which did not echo with Homer's language – his verse.[2]

Next in the epic ranking of influence and importance is Hesiod. Hesiod's two greatest poems, the *Theogony* and the *Works and Days* are both explicitly didactic: they set out to teach and were read and recited as such. The *Theogony* narrates the history of the gods and how the different divinities of the polytheistic system interreact and enter the world of men. The *Works and Days* links advice on farming to an extended plea for the value of justice in society. The *Theogony* represents a world full of gods; the *Works and Days* struggles with man's difficult physical and social life in that world. It is telling that Herodotus states that Hesiod and Homer were the foundational texts of Greek *religion*: these poets are the acknowledged legislators of a world view.[3]

The performance of poetry was absolutely basic to the social fabric of archaic culture. Religious festivals included hymns; recitals of Homer in competitive or more relaxed form were also usually preceded by hymns; so too drinking parties (*symposia*) began with a song to the gods. Perhaps most significantly, however, religious and many other celebratory occasions were marked by the performance of *choral odes*. To sing and dance in a chorus required practice and training, and the learning of songs which encapsulated the stories and values of the city. Performing choruses and watching choruses helped promote and project the values of the social group as a group. Performing in a chorus was an expected part of how a citizen lived and was integrated into social life. At the same time, in the far more intimate setting of the *symposium*, men performed the sexy and brilliant lyrics of a Sappho or an Anacreon – or the more stolidly moralizing couplets of Theognis.[4]

---

[2] See e.g. Clarke (1981); Nagy (1990); Goldhill (1986), 138–67; Gould (1983) – all of whom deal with the effect of Homer in the period covered by this book.

[3] See e.g. Clay (1989); Foley (1994); Lamberton (1988); Martin (1984); Arthur (1982); Arthur (1983); Loraux (1993), 72–110; Vernant (1983).

[4] The standard work here is Calame (1997); on Theognis, Figueira and Nagy edd. (1985); on performance and epic, Nagy (1979); on sympotics, Murray ed. (1990); Stehle (1997).

At the most public, political level it was still verse and its performance that counted. Solon led Athens out of political crisis at the end of the sixth century – he is often taken as a founding father of democracy. Central to the story of Solon is the anecdote that the turning point of his political career was when he recited his poems in the market-place to the Athenians. The historical truth of the anecdote is not important: it testifies to the importance of the place of performance of poetry in the political imagination of the Athenians. And – above all – Solon's poems remain prime sources for the politics of the period.[5]

At the opposite extreme of public and private experience of verse (and we are probably already in the first years of the fifth century now), there is the extraordinary poem of Parmenides, usually known as the 'Way of Seeming' and the 'Way of Truth'. Parmenides explores the nature of Being itself and develops an argument which has obsessed philosophers from Plato to Heidegger – in the same form of hexameter verse as used by Homer. The most complex and profound argument about the nature of reality comes in verse form.[6]

In short, whether you turn to politics or to the most intense intellectual enquiry, whether you talk of war or sex, religion or travel, moral advice or subsistence farming, any text of importance is produced in poetry – and the performance of verse runs through archaic culture not just as a leisure activity but as the medium for intellectually and socially privileged exchange.

There is, then, an extensive tradition of *authoritative* expression being formulated in poetry long before there is any evidence of any serious or lengthy work in prose. The only counterweight to this tradition is the beginnings of Greek law. Although inscriptions of any length survive mainly from the fifth and fourth centuries (and more recent periods, of course), these contain material which appears to have a longer history. As the *polis* becomes a polity – a city with a constitution – prose seems to have been the language of the formulation of such founding laws.[7] In the fifth-century city, and especially in democratic Athens, however, there is a remarkable cultural sea-change. It is not as though poetry disappears in the fifth-century enlightenment. Far from it. Not only is Homer

---

[5] For the basic facts see Forrest (1966), 143–81; Osborne (1996), 220–5.

[6] For text and translation see Kirk, Raven and Schofield (1983) and, for further discussion with bibliography, Barnes (1979), 155–230.

[7] The best general introduction is Gagarin (1986); see Snodgrass (1980), 118–22 for the rapid spread of law codes; for the general question of oral/written material, see Thomas (1989); for general questions of Greek law see Foxhall and Lewis edd. (1996); Cartledge, Millett and Todd (1990); Osborne (1985).

regularly recited – in full at the Athenian festival of the Great
Panathenaia – but also tragedy and comedy (both, of course, in verse)
are lasting innovations of the democratic city, public occasions of
immense cultural significance which rapidly entered the education
system and the imagination of the Greek-speaking world.[8] *Symposia*
continued to echo with old and new songs, choral odes were sung at
festivals and more private celebrations. In the earlier years of the fifth
century, Empedocles even continued the model of Parmenides, developing in hexameter verse his celebrated theory of the 'four roots', the
four elements, as the building blocks of matter. Nor is it the case that
there was *no* prose before the heyday of the fifth century – the Milesian
writers on the physical nature of the world, Anaximander and Anaximenes, appear to have expressed themselves in prose, and Heraclitus of
Ephesus, who criticized Homer and Hesiod, at the end of the sixth
century also wrote a book in prose which he deposited in the temple of
Artemis. The earliest laws – like the famous measures of Draco –
became adopted as foundational texts for democracy.[9] But the fifth-
century city is also the place where political theory, scientific theory, the
arts of rhetoric and of medicine, the writing of philosophy and of history
are all inaugurated.[10] This extraordinary outburst of new ways of
thinking and writing about the world is what we usually mean by the
'Greek enlightenment'. Each of these revolutionary practices is conducted in prose. Prose is the medium in which the intellectual revolution
of the enlightenment is enacted. And after the fifth century, almost all
serious philosophy, history, medicine, mathematics, theology – the
sciences of authority – are conducted solely in prose. Prose becomes a
dominant, authoritative medium from the fifth century.

This is, however, not just a revolution in wisdom – a shift in
intellectual practices alone. There is also a huge change in the institutional framework of the city. The most important political arenas in
Athenian democracy are now the Assembly and the Law Courts. In
both, men compete for status and power in the state by making
speeches. Democracy, as Demosthenes declares, is a 'constitution of
speech-making' [*politeia en logois*].[11] Writing and performing prose
becomes the key to personal position and public policy in the political
life of the city. And these public decisions were recorded in stone – in

---

[8] For tragedy, see Goldhill (1986); Easterling ed. (1997).
[9] See, on Draco, Carawan (1998).
[10] See the fundamental study of Lloyd (1987).
[11] Dem. 19. 184.

prose – on monumental pillars round the city; discussed by theorists and activists in treatises; revisited in published speeches; analysed in histories – all in prose.

Prose becomes thus the medium for authoritative expression, the expression of power. One of the arguments of this book will be that this profound shift in institutional and intellectual practice – the invention of prose – indicates a significant change in the way the relationship between man, his language and the world is conceptualized and enacted. This shift could be expressed in its most simple and dramatic form as the move from the scene of a divinely inspired bard singing the poetry of the Muses for a spell-bound audience, to the scene of two orators, arguing a legal case in front of an appointed group of judging citizens. Such dramatic images are always seductive; but, as we will see, this social and conceptual development is far more complex than such simple images can capture – and far more interesting. For the moment, it will be enough to say that the invention of prose is not just the discovery of a technique nor just the formalization of everyday speech, but a cultural development integral to the most important political and intellectual crises around the birth of democracy and the revolutions of wisdom of the classical city – crises of which we are all cultural descendants.

Prose does not have it all its own way, however, in Greece or elsewhere in the ancient or modern world. It's not just that there are important, authoritative works of politics, science and history in verse – Lucretius will still write great philosophy in Latin hexameters, Vergil an epic of power and politics with lasting effect, Lucan a poetic history of the Roman civil war; and Aratus – in Greek – will write an astronomical treatise in verse. Rather, the divine inspiration of poetry can be turned *against* prose. As late as the second century CE, the orator Aelius Aristides feels the need to apologize for writing a hymn in prose – which he calls *pezos logos*, 'speech on foot', 'pedestrian language'.[12] To call anything 'prosaic' – even prose – is to damn it with the very faintest of praise. Poetry, however, has 'winged words', and 'soars like an eagle' – it is not earthbound, 'on foot'. Poetry can claim divine inspiration and transcendent language to trump prose's appropriation of authority.

This contest between prose and poetry has been expressed with very different emphases over the centuries. What matters for me here is the recognition that the invention of prose involves a *contest of authority*.

---

[12] Aelius Aristides 45 [*To Serapis*]. 8, where he also calls prose 'natural'.

How does a prose author claim authority for what he says? And how does the writer of prose find space for his work in the contest of voices that make up the democratic city? The new writers of the new form of prose need to compete for (discursive) space in the city, and one of the major aims of this book will be to trace the ways that this struggle is conducted.

There are three chapters that follow, each of which deals with a major genre of the new writing of the classical city. The first looks at history, and the historians Herodotus and Thucydides. Why does telling the story of the past matter? How does this new genre handle the problem of multiple versions of the past and the need to create an authoritative account? The second and central chapter considers rhetoric – both the science and the practice of oratory. What difference does the formal study of techniques of argument make? How does an orator present himself as authoritative? The third chapter looks at philosophy and science, especially Plato's dialogues and Aristotle's treatises. How does philosophy claim a special status for its techniques over and against poetry and rhetoric? What makes scientific analysis convincing? How does philosophy strive towards science?

I have formally separated these three areas for discussion because they represent what will become major genres of prose writing. But it must not be forgotten that the overlaps between these fields are constant and fascinating. In particular, the science of rhetoric becomes a mainstay of education in the city. Since making speeches is a key route to power, studying how to make good speeches is an education that promises status, influence, success. Because rhetoric becomes a normal part of education, its influence is evident in the writing of all the authors in the ancient world. Similarly, though in a more restricted way, Thucydides adopts the language of medicine and science; the medical writers reflect philosophically on their own methods; Plato's dialogues echo with the mix of languages which makes up the babble of the intellectual city; Aristotle philosophizes about rhetoric, science, history – and poetry. You could say that my first chapter looks at the rhetoric of History, the second at the rhetoric of Rhetoric, and the third at the rhetoric of Philosophy.

The following chapters focus on particular areas largely for ease and clarity of exposition: but it is the interrelation between these areas – the invention of *prose* – that is the quarry of my research. Consequently, I will end this introduction with a paragraph from a prose work which sums up not only the revolutionary status of prose but also the overlap of different types of writing. It is a paragraph from a fifth-century treatise called *Airs, Waters, Places*. This text, transmitted in the medical writings known as the Hippocratic Corpus, is a geographical and ecological treatise on how the environment affects social and political development. It looks at how the quality of the atmosphere, water supply, and other factors of physical surroundings effect the physical health and behaviour of various communities. This paragraph is a transitional section in the discussion of the different qualities of Europe and Asia:

> That is how it is, then, with regard to the difference in nature [*phusis*] and shape between Asiatics and Europeans. With regard to lack of spirit and lack of manliness, the most important reason [*aitiai*][13] why the Asiatics are less warlike and more gentle in character, is the seasons, which show no great change in heat or cold, but are all similar. For there are no traumas of mind nor strong bodily change, which are likely [*eikos*] to steel the temper and to produce passion and spirit more than monotonous consistency. For it is changes in all manner of things which stimulate the mind and prevent it from stagnating. From these reasons it seems to me that the Asiatic race [*genos*] is weak; and their institutions [*nomoi*] also contribute. For most of Asia is ruled by kings. Where men are not their own masters and autonomous, but have a master, their rationale [*logos*] is not to practise the arts of war, but to avoid seeming good fighters.   (*Airs, Waters, Places* 16)

The opening sentence demonstrates a scientific requirement of abstraction and generalization. What has been described, he concludes, is the 'difference in nature and shape between Asiatics and Europeans'. The word *phusis* – 'nature' – occurs only once in Homer (to describe how a plant grows); but it is a buzz word of the fifth century, a principle of investigation and exploration.[14] It is usually opposed to *nomos*, convention or law, and indeed the final sentences specify that Asiatic weakness is also due precisely to their *nomoi* – or 'institutions', as I have translated it – that is, their government by monarchy. 'Asia' and 'Europe' as categories also indicate a new way of conceiving the world. The Persian invasion of Greece in the fifth century was instrumental in fostering a Panhellenic self-recognition of Greekness as opposed to merely an affiliation with an individual city or realm.[15] The 'barbarian' as the excluded and derided other becomes a commonplace of Greek thinking, which also led, as here, to more extensive and

---

[13] *Aitiai* is the plural of the noun *aitiê*, which means basically 'cause' or 'reason'. The adjective *aitios* means 'responsible', 'causing'. I have transliterated the noun or the adjective as appropriate, in the form in which they appear in the various texts quoted.

[14] The standard work is in German (Heinimann [1945]), but there is a useful introduction in Guthrie (1962–81) vol. III, 55ff. See also below, pp. 48–9. More general and interesting is Farrar (1988); for a political account of the role of *nomos* see Ostwald (1986); on Herodotus see Humphreys (1987).

[15] For the 'invention of the barbarian', see Hall (1989); Hartog (1988); Miller (1997).

complex racial thinking. *Airs, Waters, Places* requires of its reader a
broad conceptualization of racial identity – which attempts to explain by
scientific analysis differences between cultures. The key term is *aitios*,
'responsible', 'causal', or *aitia*, 'cause', 'reason'. To seek for the cause of
things is a foundational gesture of the new self-reflexive scientific
thinking (as we will see repeatedly in the chapters that follow). Here,
the causes considered are the patterning of the seasons which produce
different reactions. The bland similarity of Asiatic weather cannot
sharpen and harden the spirit in the way that the harsh extremes of
European weather can. This is not just a piece of folkloric wisdom, but is
expressed in the technical language of meteorology and physiology: the
Asiatics do not experience *ekplêxis* of the mind, nor *metastasis* of the
body. Yet the final turn of the argument is to political theory. Monarchy
is a cause of military weakness, because (as the paragraph will continue
in detail) being ruled by a single man rather than being autonomous has
a bad effect on military training, bravery and commitment. The bravery
and military prowess which dominate the values of epic are now
theorized as a symptom of a political constitution.

This passage, then, links its political and scientific theorizing with a
historical and physiological explanation of Asiatic feebleness. It
expresses its argument in balanced and opposed clauses (*peri men . . .
peri de*, 'with regard to . . . with regard to'), balanced and opposed
vocabulary (*phusis/nomos*, 'nature'/'law', *gnômê/sôma*, 'mind'/'body',
'Asiatic'/'European'). It links its arguments causally – the repeated
use of *gar*, 'for' – and it utilizes the abstract idea of 'probability',
'likelihood' [*eikos*] to allow its generalization to deal with exceptional
cases. It shows, that is, the organization and expressions of a rhetorically informed language of explanation. What is more, it marks its
novelty and the authority of its writer by the addition of *emoi dokei*, 'it
seems to me'. It is the author and nature who together structure this
case. This argument about racial strength and feebleness is a long way
from a Homeric picture, where the *gods* fill Hector or Achilles with
strength.

This paragraph shows clearly how the new prose brings to bear
scientific enquiry and theorizing about politics and the physical world,
in order to explore in rhetorically trained language a view of the world –
a world articulated by explicit, general and abstract principles – nature,
race, likelihood – and centered on man as agent in the world. This prose
does not unfurl like a divinely inspired poem poured through the lips of
the bard; it is organized and produced by a self-consciously analytical

and persuasive subject who proclaims his mastery of knowledge. It wants to change the way you see the world.

It is the excitement and power of this revolutionary way of writing the world that this book hopes to demonstrate.

II. HISTORY: AUTHORITY THROUGH NARRATIVE

Herodotus was not the first to write prose. When his *History* appeared, probably in the 430s BCE, the scientists of Ionia (like the author of *Airs, Waters, Places*) had been working for more than a generation. Anaximander and Anaximenes had produced works on the nature of the world as early as the middle of the sixth century, and Hecataeus had already produced his *Periodos Gês*, 'Trip around the World', which surveyed the nations of the Mediterranean. Heraclitus had deposited his paradoxical provocations in the temple of Artemis at Ephesus.[1] Yet, both for the Greeks and for us, what Herodotus achieved demands to be seen as a radical departure. For the first time, the stirring and dramatic events of a nation at war are not merely recorded but explored and discussed at epic length in prose. It is extremely difficult after the long history of History to appreciate just how remarkable this innovative and foundational act is.

In the aftermath of the unexpected and heroic defeat of Persia, the Greek-speaking world was experiencing rapid and tumultuous social and cultural change. Athens was in the process of developing a fully democratic political system, and extending its power through the Eastern Mediterranean thanks to its immense fleet.[2] Sparta, Corinth and the other Greek cities observed – or suffered from – this imperialist expansion with considerable concern (which led ultimately to the Peloponnesian War). The wealth that stemmed from the empire changed the city of Athens with the construction of an architecture of empire – the Parthenon, the Painted Stoa and the other buildings covered with the images of Athenian power.[3] The great institutions of democracy – the Assembly, the courts, the festivals of tragedy and comedy, the Panathenaia's games and competitions – required the active participation of its citizens and attracted huge numbers of foreign visitors – ambassadors, tourists, writers, performers . . .[4] The funda-

---

[1] The testimonia on these early writers are most easily found in Kirk, Raven and Schofield (1983); Hecataeus in Jacoby's *Fragments of the Greek Historians*.

[2] Forrest (1966) and Davies (1993) are brief and still useful introductions; a much more detailed account is Ostwald (1986), and an up-to-date introduction is Osborne ed. (2000). Hornblower (1991) usefully goes well beyond Athens.

[3] See Pollitt (1972); Osborne (1987); Castriota (1992); Rhodes (1995); Osborne (1998): looking at the politics of Greek art has become standard now.

[4] On festivals and their culture, see Goldhill (1986), (2000); Connor (1987); Osborne (1993); Neils ed. (1992); Goldhill and Osborne edd. (1999) – all with extensive further bibliography.

mental shifts in intellectual perspective during this era are the subject of this book, and Herodotus stands at the head of my discussion because of his iconic project of explaining the war that had made all this possible. For the ancient world and for modern thinking, Herodotus is 'the father of history'.

So how does Herodotus start (his) history? Here's the first sentence:

This is the display of the research of Herodotus of Halicarnassus, made so that human achievements should not fade with time, and so that great and wondrous deeds displayed by Greeks and barbarians should not be without lasting fame: my particular concern is the reason they went to war with one another.

The first word in Greek is *Herodotou*, the name of the author. This immediately marks the difference between this history and, say, Homeric epic. Homer's name does not appear in his works at all, and self-reference is limited to the invocation to the Muses to sing to 'me, too'. Even Hesiod's name occurs only in the context of the Muses teaching him to sing.[5] Here the whole history is placed under the aegis of its human agent, who proudly declares himself, first word. Protagoras, the sophist, famously declared that 'man is the measure of all things'.[6] This account of the past has a firmly announced human origin and authority.

The second word is 'of Halicarnassus'.[7] Does it matter where you come from – and in what ways? We have already seen how *Airs, Waters, Places* theorizes the importance of environment, but a history is always written from a stance, especially the history of war, with the inevitable slanting of a victor's or victim's tale. Halicarnassus is on the Ionian coast, in the centre of the territory associated with the birth of Greek science, a town which marks the heavily contested boundary between the Greek world and the Persian Empire. Herodotus' history will not be a narrowly circumscribed account of battles of invasion, but also a tour round the Mediterranean exploring the cultural basis of the clash between East and West. The location 'of Halicarnassus' signals a position – writing on the boundary between Greece and its enemy.

---

[5] On the thematics of naming in Homer see Goldhill (1991), ch. 1; and on the nature of the name of Hesiod and of Homer, Nagy (1979), 296–300; (1990), 52–82, who puts a strong case for the generic (rather than individual) value of both names.

[6] An interesting version of Protagoras and democracy in Farrar (1988), 44–125.

[7] Aristotle *Rhet.* 3. 9. 2 (mis)quotes this first line interestingly as 'Herodotus of Thurii'. Thurii was a new town which had laws drawn up for it by Protagoras, and was where Lysias also spent much time. Herodotus also spent time there and, according to tradition, died and was buried there. No modern editor follows Aristotle's version, though it is sometimes assumed that there was another tradition of text with such a reading. The word order is also different in Aristotle.

The next word is *historiês* – from which the modern term 'history' is derived. But *historiê* means 'enquiry', 'investigation' or, as translated above, 'research'. It is a strikingly contemporary word which links Herodotus' approach to the scientific methodological discussions of Hippocratic medicine and of physics, and it suggests an enquiry into nature and into the nature of man in an extended sense.[8] It implies the practice of collecting, sifting and evaluating evidence – rather than any divinely inspired performance. It marks Herodotus' project as intellectually self-conscious and critical. So too *apodexis*, the fourth word, 'display', or 'presentation', is not a term to be found in Homer or other archaic writers. It encapsulates a different context of performance, a different contract between audience and historian. The new intellectuals known as sophists were celebrated for their set-piece rhetorical displays, often on paradoxical subjects, which were delivered often to large audiences. Such a speech was known as an *epideixis* (and by Aristotle's *Rhetoric* it was enshrined as one branch of the art of rhetoric).[9] Herodotus invokes such a rhetorical model. As we will see, this early prose work harks back to the scene of poetic performance and forward to rhetorical display in a manner avoided by the more austere writers such as Thucydides or Aristotle. The story that Herodotus read aloud his history at Olympia at the Games – whether true or false – picks up on this performative element of the history's opening.

So, the first phrase, 'this is the display of the research of Herodotus of Halicarnassus' is a bold declaration of a revolutionary approach to writing. This is a self-conscious, critical exploration and presentation of what an individual man can find out by his intellectual effort. The sentence continues with the purpose of the history and the first statement of its subject – and both elements are carefully articulated against the paradigm of archaic epic. His purpose is expressed first in very general terms 'that human achievements should not fade over time', and then in a parallel clause with more specificity 'that the great and wondrous deeds displayed by Greeks and barbarians should not be without lasting fame'. The aim of history is to memorialize and celebrate the works of man. Herodotus' 'display' is of the deeds 'displayed' by men. On the one hand, this clearly echoes the claims of epic poetry: Achilles' purpose in fighting is to win everlasting fame [*kleos aphthiton*];

---

[8] There is much discussion of this term: the most recent and useful is Thomas (2000), which has extensive bibliography to earlier discussions.

[9] See in general Goldhill and Osborne edd. (1999), 3–4; Lloyd (1987); Thomas (2000,) 249–69 for the connections with medicine in particular.

he himself sings outside his tent about the fame of men, and the *Iliad* is the instantiation of Achilles' fame, every time it is read.[10] Herodotus' *History* aims to prevent the great deeds of men from being 'without lasting fame' [*aklea*]. He is taking over epic's *raison d'être*, especially here in the context of great deeds of war. On the other hand, his human focus is markedly different from Homer's framework. Not only are history's deeds the great and amazing acts of *men* ('great and wondrous' is an obvious encouragement to the reader to read on and be amazed), but also the humans are specified as 'Greeks and barbarians' – the difference between which it will be the history's work to explore. In Homer, the Trojans speak Greek, have the same gods as the Greeks, the same customs and values: the war is not a clash of cultures.[11] Herodotus will define this war as a struggle about cultural identity. Finally, to end this first sentence, he specifies his main theme: 'the reason [*aitiê*] they went to war with one another'. The buzz word *aitiê*, 'cause', 'reason' looks back to *historiês*: the enquiry is to investigate the causes and not merely the events of war. 'Who started the quarrel?', asks Homer at the beginning of the *Iliad*, and immediately answers, 'Leto's son, Apollo'.[12] Similarly when Helen appears on the walls of Troy, Priam comments 'I do not hold you responsible [*aitiê*]; the gods are responsible [*aitioi*] for the war'.[13] This form of explanation can be heard behind Herodotus' approach – but it is a model he dismisses in the name of human agency and the complexity of multiple causes – cultural, political, intellectual. Where Homer asks and answers the question of cause with a swift and divine solution, Herodotus maintains causality as the foundational *problem* of history.

I have gone through the first sentence in this detail to show just how carefully expressive it is, and how its outlook is poised between its radical innovation and its competition with past models of epic memorialization. The following paragraphs of his introduction – which I will not be able to look at word by word here! – brilliantly articulate his foundational problem of causality by immediately introducing us to different stories of the past and different ways of telling those stories. He begins with a rapid account of what Persian authorities say on the matter:

[10] For discussion and bibliography see Goldhill (1991), chapter 2.
[11] Later writers, however, certainly saw the Trojans as barbarians, and Mackie (1996) makes the strongest case for significant differences between Greeks and Trojans. See, however, Hall (1989) and Redfield (1975).
[12] *Il.* 1. 8–9.
[13] *Il.* 3. 164.

Persian experts [*logioi*] say that the Phoenicians are the cause [*aitioi*] of the difference. For they . . .

Here is a first version of the *aitia* of war, given by the Persians who profess authority in the matter of such old tales.[14] Their story is that the Phoenicians went to Argos to trade, and when they left they took with them some women including the king's daughter. This girl is known to the Persians and Greeks as Io. This led the Greeks to snatch Europa from Tyre in revenge. But the Greeks themselves were responsible for a further breach because they went to Phasis and snatched Medea – which was used as an excuse by Alexander, that is, Paris, Priam's son, when he seized Helen. These were all single acts of abduction. The Greeks were responsible [*aitioi*], however, for a drastic escalation of military activity when they sent a full army against Asia to recapture Helen – an act regarded by Persians as out of all proportion to the cause.

This is a remarkable narrative.[15] First of all, the pattern of rape and revenge is told in a relentlessly rationalist manner: that is, there is no place in the stories of Io and Europa for the familiar Greek mythic models of Zeus in the shape of a bull carrying off Europa, or Io being turned into a cow by Hera and pursued by a gadfly. These are tales of trade and sordid sexual advantage. Helen is just a snatched girl: there is no mention of the judgement of Paris or any other part of the mythical apparatus with which the story is invested in Greek accounts. Medea brings no Golden Fleece; there is no Argo with its crew of heroes. What is more, each of these tales is also familiar from some of the grandest and most powerful of Greek literature. Here, each tale is barely and briefly told with scarcely an adjective or adverb, let alone the complexity and power of epic or tragic verse. At one level, then, this passage reduces the epic tradition of Greece to a dismissive paragraph. But the whole account is offered as what the Persian experts say: that this is the version of these *logioi* – masters of tales – is emphasized by a constant repetition of 'they say', 'so they put it'. The account ends 'that's what the Persians say happened and they find that the beginning of their hatred towards the Greeks is because of the capture of Troy' – but immediately adds that the Phoenicians do not agree about Io. Herodotus is setting us in the midst of competing national versions of early history, each of which offers a simple – indeed totally oversimplified – account of how the East

[14] On the sense of *logioi* see Nagy (1987).
[15] On Herodotean narrative in general see Lang (1984); Immerwahr (1966); and from a different, less unitarian perspective Fornara (1971); Marincola (2001). On this passage see e.g. Fowler (1996); Pelliccia (1992), which set it in a context.

and West came into conflict. The pattern of cause and effect – *aitia* – is so naive that it is hard not to see Herodotus constructing a parodic countermodel for his own extended and intricate cultural analyses to follow. The Persian experts, it seems, don't *get* history.

The transition is strongly marked:

> About these things I am not come to say that they happened like this or in some other way. Rather, the person I myself know to have begun the crimes against the Greeks I will indicate and advance to . . .

The tales of the Persian experts and the Phoenicians are indeed just a foil to to the authoritative knowledge of the Greek historian. Instead of the claim and counterclaim of the simplistic *logioi*, Herodotus promises that he will start from the firm basis of declaring the name of the man who can be known certainly to have committed crimes against the Greeks – and the first word of the next paragraph is 'Croesus . . .', the famously rich ruler who conquered the Ionian seaboard. The story of Croesus that follows, unlike the story of the *logioi*, stretches out over many pages, involves different time frames, discusses the power of the gods, and offers a powerful dramatic portrayal, complete with dialogue and moral conclusion.[16] There are different ways to tell stories and to do history, and Herodotus tellingly juxtaposes the Persian experts to his own mastery.

The opening section of Herodotus' *Histories*, then, sets Herodotus' version of the Persian version of the conflict with Greece in the frame of the historian's self-representation as intellectual master, evaluating evidence, choosing a line of narrative, directing and encouraging the reader to follow him on his new epic journey. The following sections of my chapter will each pick up one of the themes established by this remarkable beginning: first, Greeks and barbarians – or 'us and them'. How is Herodotus' opening presentation of Greeks looking at Persians looking at Greeks further explored in his series of brilliant cultural excursuses? Second, the promised wonders: how do geographical and other marvels fit into Herodotus' scheme? Third, techniques or strategies of projecting and maintaining the authority of the historian: how does the historian, amid the competing versions of the past, establish his persuasiveness?

---

[16] On Croesus see Gould (1989), who draws on Segal (1971); Stahl (1975) and Sebeok and Brady (1979); Moles (1996).

II

Herodotus' *Histories* recounts the Greek victories over the Persian invaders in 490 and 480 BCE. The crucial battles of these two campaigns – Marathon, Thermopylae, Salamis, Plataea – are not discussed until Book VI – two thirds of the way through. The first books explore the *aitiai* – the causes – of the war in the very broadest possible way. This involves not merely the rise to power of Darius and his successor, Xerxes, or the preparations for invasion, but also and more importantly a kaleidoscopic portrayal of what makes the Greeks Greek and the Persians Persian. Herodotus sees this war as a clash of cultures, a 'conflict about everything', as Aeschylus famously puts it in the *Persians*, his tragedy about the same victory.[17] This war is indeed a turning point in Greek self-definition and in the construction of the idea of the barbarian: it is only with the conflict with Persia that the generalizing cultural ideal of 'the Greeks' – *hoi Hellênes* – becomes a dominant unifying concept for the different cities and islands of the Greek-speaking world. No figure is more significant than Herodotus in this development of Greek self-representation.[18]

Herodotus provides a telling set of images of the East for Greek readers. This can take the form of a list of the twenty provinces of the Persian Empire and the tribute each pays to the crown – a list that is not merely informative but also stresses the wealth and size of the Empire against which Greece is pitted.[19] (At the time Herodotus published, it also would remind its Athenian readers of their own tribute and empire.) Or it could take the form of the description of a strangely different ritual practice over there, or a bizarre reversal of Greek social practice in one of the outposts of that kingdom – sex in the streets, women in charge, burying the dead in honey.[20] It can take the form of telling the story of the Persian past: the childhood of Cyrus the Great – the boy sent to live with cowherds till his own royal nature emerged; the extraordinary rise to power of Darius, overthrowing the Magi who had seized power; the collapse of the rule of Croesus, after he received the oracle that told him a great kingdom would fall if he

---

[17] Aesch. *Pers.* 405, to be read with the commentary of Hall (1996).
[18] See Gould (1989) – still the best introduction to Herodotus; also Hall (1989); Romm (1998); Cartledge (1993); and the more detailed Hartog (1988).
[19] Her. 3. 91.
[20] For this sense of reversal see Pembroke (1967); Vidal-Naquet (1981).

went to war – and, assuming it meant his enemies' land, marched off to self-destruction. In particular, however, it is also Herodotus' brilliant persuasive use of cultural imagery that creates 'the barbarian'. His representation of the East's great wealth and terrifying power, linked to dangerous femininity and its dominance by monarchical rulers, scarred by treacherous and arrogant behaviour, gives us fundamental elements of what has been a very long history of the West's image of the Oriental other.[21]

Herodotus, however, also shows the Persians finding out about the Greeks. He dramatizes Xerxes, as he musters his huge army, asking Demaratus, a Greek, whether the Greeks would dare fight such a force, and receives a wonderful eulogy of Spartan excellence in reply: 'Fighting together, they are the best soldiers in the world. They are free – yes – but not entirely free. For they have a master, namely, the Law, which they fear more than your subjects fear you. They do whatever that lord commands, and it commands always the same thing: never to flee in battle, however great the enemy, but to stand firm, to conquer or to perish'.[22] Xerxes receives this speech with a good-humoured laugh[23] – but these words are recalled before Thermopylae, where three hundred Spartans prepare to hold off the might of the Persian empire. It is reported to Xerxes that the Spartans are carefully combing and arranging their hair. 'This is their custom', explains Demaratus, 'before risking their lives'. Xerxes cannot believe him – and his army suffers terrible losses.[24] The king is forced to learn that 'he had many people in his army, but few real men'.

The Persians are forced to learn of Greek excellence, then, as the Greek audience revels in victory (and learns of the oddness of Persian ways). It might seem therefore that the opposition of Greeks and Persians in the *Histories* is wholly slanted towards the Greeks. Herodotus, however, although he writes as a Greek for Greeks, constructs a far more complex and subtle narrative than such a gung-ho bias might suggest. There is, first of all, extensive praise for the early Persians who could indeed match Greek rigour and hardness; there is also a sympathetic relativism that recognizes not so much the evident priority of Greek customs as the conventionality of all social norms. Each nation, in Herodotus, has its own ways and gods. Indeed, Plutarch, writing in the

---

[21] Said (1978) has been massively influential here.
[22] Her. 7. 104. On Demaratus, see Boedeker (1987).
[23] On the narrative use of laughter in Herodotus see Lateiner (1977).
[24] Her. 7. 209.

first century CE, is so riled by the careful sympathies of Herodotus that he writes a treatise accusing him of being a *philobarbaros* – a 'barbarian lover'.[25]

There are three particularly relevant ways in which the potentially stark polarity of Greek and barbarian is manipulated, explored and complicated. First, both Greek and Persian as general categories are repeatedly fissured into different Greek and Persian cities, times, attitudes. Demaratus praises the Spartans as the best of the Greeks, and their military and social qualities are treated at some length; but other Greek cities too, notably Athens and Corinth and the cities of the Ionian seaboard are portrayed in some detail. The Medes and other tribes of the Persian empire are delineated and distinguished from the Persian court. This leads to the second and more far-reaching narrative strategy. For Greece and Persia are repeatedly set not merely in opposition to each other, but are viewed also through the lens of other major cultures. So, for example, much of Book II is devoted to Egypt. Egypt is said by Herodotus to be a much older culture than Greece and with a range of knowledge and expertise before which Greece can only appear as a Johnny-come-lately.[26] As we will see in the next section, Herodotus' geographical and anthropological observations do not merely shock or titillate the Greek reader with the exoticism of the other but also expose the pretensions of Greek cultural superiority. Greek claims of superiority are laughable in the context of Egyptian antiquity, writes Herodotus, and even the gods of Greece are imports from Egypt.[27] Similarly, there is a fascinating representation of the nomads of Scythia. When these nomads are attacked by Persia, they demonstrate social qualities of bravery, intelligence and resistance that link them easily to models of Greek heroism. When they come into contact with Greeks, however, their nomadic lifestyle, their liaison with fierce female warriors, the Amazons, their reliance on horses, all distinguish them from the crop-growing, city-dwelling, marriage-loving Greeks. The Scythians act as a shifting mirror in which positive and negative aspects of Greek and Persian culture are reflected.[28]

Indeed, Herodotus travels right round the Mediterranean mapping

---

[25] Plutarch, *On the Malignity of Herodotus*.

[26] The best general account of Herodotus 'abroad' is Redfield (1985); see also Lloyd (1990). There is much discussion of the truth or value of Herodotus' Egyptian account: most dismissive is Fehling (1989); most credulous is Bernal (1987); more interesting is Hunter (1982), 50–92.

[27] The most up-to-date book on Herodotus' religion is Harrison (2000), though it has been widely criticized for undervaluing the sophistication of Herodotus' account.

[28] Hartog's brilliant account has been seminal in Herodotean studies (Hartog [1988]).

the variables of cultural difference. This can be explored with bold and surprising humour ('The Lydians have similar customs to the Greeks – except they prostitute their daughters'[29]); with off-hand – but never casual – detail ('The Atlantes are said to eat no living creature and never to dream'[30]); or with more extensive histories and critical investigation. Every element contributes towards understanding and evaluating cultural norms. The positive and negative images construct a kaleidoscope – a shifting patterning of mirrors – in which Greekness is viewed and critically reflected on. The boundaries of the normal are not so much asserted as explored through variation after variation of *nomos* (custom/convention/law). What it means to be Greek rather than Persian becomes a question, an investigation rather than a triumphant assertion. It is common to call these anthropological and geographical descriptions 'digressions' – and Herodotus himself notes explicitly that they are not an obvious part of the narrative of war.[31] But they play an absolutely integral role in the *aitia* of war – the explanation of how Greek and Persian cultures came into conflict.

The third way in which the polarity of Greek and barbarian escapes from naive or jingoistic opposition is the most polemical. Herodotus is writing some forty to fifty years after the events he describes and he was composing still when the Peloponnesian War started at the height of the expansion of the Athenian Empire. An Athenian audience is to be expected for the *Histories*, both because of the anecdotal tradition that Herodotus worked in Athens, and because so many writers and thinkers from outside Athens visited what was the most important centre for intellectual activity in the Greek world. The history of Herodotus is set, as we have seen, under the aegis of the mutability of human fortune, and specifically the rise and fall of empires. The self-confidence and collapse of the Persian imperial policy might therefore be taken as a model – a worrying or critical question – for Athens itself.

Persia, then, as a *lesson* for Greeks? Consider one of the most famous passages of the *Histories*, the so-called debate of the constitutions.[32] Darius, the father of Xerxes, comes to power in Persia after a violent conspiracy against the Magi, the priests. The seven conspirators meet after the success of their plot to decide how Persia is to be ruled. Otabanes speaks first on behalf of democracy – in favour of open debate, equality before the law, and accountability of officials to

---

[29] Her. 1. 94.   [30] Her. 4. 184.   [31] Her. 4. 30.
[32] Her. 3. 80–4. For discussions of Herodotean politics, see Fornara (1971); Raaflaub (1987), Gould (1989), 116–20; Moles (1996).

the people. Megabyzus speaks on behalf of oligarchy – that a group of the best men will produce the best decisions and avoid both the fickleness of the mob and the arbitrariness and irresponsibility of a tyrant. Darius, speaking third, argues for monarchy. If the best man is chosen, how could one better the rule of a single person, in control of himself and not open to the rivalries and dissension of group rule or the oscillating power plays of democracy and oligarchy? The remaining conspirators vote in agreement with Darius, and Persia becomes a monarchy.

Now Herodotus goes to some pains to insist that this story is true, in a way which flags the problem of belief so patently that an especially close engagement seems to be called for: 'these speeches *were* delivered – unbelievable though that is to some Greeks – but delivered they were'.[33] The problem is not just the surprisingly formal process of debate but the fact that the Persian conspirators adopt the standard Greek definitions of political systems and the standard terms of Greek political discussion. This language, however, *engages* the Athenian reader in a fascinating process of self-recognition. The passage poses politically-loaded questions: to what degree does a political constitution determine historical narrative? What would – could – have happened if the conspirators had made another choice? Can a Persian democracy, for example, be imagined? How is Athenian democracy – as opposed to, say, Spartan rule – to be 'chosen'? And more besides. Herodotus' *History* offers a stimulating arena for contemporary political reflection in which Persian power and its narratives are not simply the excluded or derided negation of Greek politics but a more intricate, subtle and provocative evaluative model with which to do political thinking.

Herodotus' *History*, then, offers a highly complex map not just of the conflict between Greeks and Persians but also of other cultures: it is a map which encourages the reader to place himself or herself within a matrix of social, moral and political markers. It is a map on which Greeks are to locate and explore their cultural identity. The invention of prose here is also a fundamental element in the story of the invention of Greekness.

---

[33] Her. 3. 80.

III

'Wonder' is what occurs when a Homeric character is faced by exceptional beauty, size, outlandishness – or by the marvels of the physical world. Wonder is the emotional response to something that goes beyond the expected – and thus it articulates the boundaries of the (ab)normal. The common formula in Homer, 'a wonder to behold', or its equivalent, 'he saw and wondered', is prompted, for example, when Hermes gazes at Calypso's verdant island, or when Odysseus sees the city of the Phaeacians, or when Priam turns up unannounced in Achilles' tent at night.[34] In Homeric epic, the pursuit of excellence is framed by an audience's recognition of the outstanding which is marked by the expression of wonder. But response to wonder is celebration or an awestruck silence; rarely, if ever, a move towards explanation. For Homer, gods fill a man with strength or endow a woman with beauty, and the reaction of humans is awe. For the historian and philosopher of the classical city, however, wonder provokes a desire to know, followed by research, hypothesis and argument. As Aristotle put it, 'For humans, wonder is the beginning of philosophy'.[35] This is not merely a generic shift from epic to history or philosophy, but the discovery of nature – *phusis* – as an object of enquiry. As we saw in the introduction, now the very air breathed and water drunk are open to investigation and require the mastery of human knowledge. Wonder now provokes the study of *aitiai*.

Herodotus is poised at the turning-point of this history of wonder. The philosophical poems of Parmenides and Empedocles have already opened the nature of reality to exploration, the Ionian scientists have already begun to theorize about the nature of matter, doctors about the body. Herodotus too is keen to turn an analytic gaze at what he sees, and to stake a position in the competitive market of explanation. Yet when the prologue of the *History* promises *erga thaumasta*, 'wondrous', 'amazing deeds', he is also looking back towards the epic achievements of the heroes of the Trojan war, and promising stories and facts to amaze the reader.

Herodotus explains that he has extended his account of Egypt because it has more 'wondrous things' [*thaumasia*] than other countries

---

[34] *Od.* 5. 74; *Od.* 7.43–5; *Il.* 24. 483–4: the full range of the language of wonder and sight is discussed by Prier (1989).
[35] Arist. *Met.* 1. 2. 9 (982b).

and so needs more discussion [*logos*].[36] Some of these wonders are listed without much attempt at analysis. Flying snakes (not with feathered wings, but with the wings of a bat) are eaten by the ibis – the black ibis, not the bald ibis. There are ants, bigger than foxes but smaller than dogs, who dig gold.[37] Like the tribe who copulate in public or the Atlantes who do not dream, these wonders are presented as bare facts. Yet these amazements are not merely to enthrall an audience – wonderful though they are to read. First, as I will discuss in the next section in more detail, Herodotus produces an array of authorial comments on the status of such facts. Some are presented as bare information, others are offered as the evidence of what Herodotus has actually seen for himself; some are presented as the stories of the Egyptians, sometimes with the corroboration of Greek or other sources, others discussed with barely concealed disbelief. There are two particularly relevant implications of this. On the one hand, the description of the world is constantly framed as the product of human investigation, doubt and judgement. The uncontested omniscience of a Muse-led Homer is replaced by a narrator who is an observer struggling for mastery, judging, estimating and passing on what he has heard from other humans, stamped with the dubious authority of hearsay, buttressed by the authority of the eye-witness. On the other hand, Herodotus represents a natural world which is open to – and even requires – such an analytic perception, if it is to be understood properly. The world needs analysis for its structure to be comprehensively articulated. Herodotus' representation of the wonders of the world in this way is science in action.

Let's take an example. Like many, Herodotus is obsessed with the Nile.[38] He describes its rising and falling, hypothesizes about its source and theorizes about what would happen if the Nile changed its flow. It is a river that is different from all others and, as it seems, the reverse of rivers elsewhere; so Egyptians are the reverse of other men. (Men urinate sitting down, women standing up; men go outside to eat, inside to defecate, and so forth with a great list of amazing facts about the Egyptians).[39] So why does the Nile flood?

Certain Greeks wishing to display their cleverness [*sophiē*], have offered three accounts of the flooding of the Nile. Two of these are not worth mentioning except to mark that they exist. One claims that Etesian winds are the cause [*aitiai*] of the river's filling

---

[36] Her. 2. 35.
[37] Ibis: Her. 2. 76. Ants: Her. 3.102.
[38] On the Nile see Vasunia (2001).
[39] See Her. 2. 35ff.

because they prevent the Nile exiting to the sea. But often the Etesian winds don't blow and the Nile behaves in the same way. What's more, if the Etesian winds were the cause [*aitiai*], the other rivers too which flow in the opposite direction to the Etesian winds would be affected in the same way as the Nile. The second explanation is less scientific than that just said; that is to say, it is more wonderful [*thaumasiôtera*]: it claims the Nile is contrived like this because it flows from Ocean, and Ocean flows round the whole world . . .The third is the most reasonable but is particularly wrong. It claims – and this is rubbish – that the Nile flows from melted snow . . .[40]

Three explanations – *aitiai* – are sniffily dismissed as the ideas of Greeks trying to show off their wisdom. The struggle in the competitive marketplace of ideas is clear here, especially in the rhetorical put-down that such notions are not really worth discussing (before he argues against them). The three reasons each require different strategies of rejection, however, according to the type of argument proposed. The first thesis is rejected on the grounds of logic, the logic that takes for granted a physical explanation is needed of a physical phenomenon. The second reason is dismissed for being rather too 'fanciful', 'wonder-ful', 'fabulous', because it predicates that the river Ocean, said to encircle the world in (e.g.) Homer's *Iliad*, is the source of the Nile. Even in an Egypt of wonders, the *explanation* of such a phenomenon must be grounded in the expectation of the normal, and not the 'mythical'. So, the third explanation is said to be 'most reasonable', *epieikestetê*, but a distinct lie. It has plausibility, unlike the other two, but is still false, and he takes some time to prove it false, before going on to offer his own account: 'if after criticizing these proposed theories I must display an opinion about these obscurities, I will indicate why in my judgement the Nile floods in summer'. And so he does.

The great wonder of the Nile is described, then, the theories about its causes discussed and evaluated, a hypothesis is offered and explored – but then with typically disarming self-irony he concludes: 'Well, enough of that: it is how it is and has been from the beginning'.[41] His own theorizing hesitates to make any bold and certain conclusion on such an obstinately obscure topic, and he lets his words hang in the air – as theorizing. Thus, even Herodotus' most scientific analysis of the most wondrous phenomenon ends with a story-teller's shrug of the shoulders, and a quick progression to the next question of the Nile's nature. It is this wonderful mixture of careful argument and open-mouthed delight in the bizarre, of apparently ingenuous reportage and spiky criticism, of

[40] Her. 2. 20.
[41] Her. 2. 28.

narrative flair and casual connection, which makes Herodotus' presentation of the wonders of the world so complex and so engaging.

The complexity of Herodotus' view of what transcends the normal is especially evident in his representation of the divine and the miraculous. The opening description of a mythic prehistory, the account of the Persian experts, was told without any divine apparatus, any 'mythic' narrative. But Herodotus' *History* is still a world full of gods. He talks repeatedly of religion and of ritual in particular, and he discusses the names and attributes of foreign and Greek gods with a challenging and polemical verve. But it is the divine as causal agency that is especially interesting for a historical narrative. In Homer, the whole narrative is introduced and summed up as the fulfilment of the plan of Zeus; the immediate cause of the conflict is Apollo; and the activities of humans at the grand and small level are motivated explicitly by divine agents. What, then, of Herodotus' *History*?

Many characters within the *History* talk of their perception of the divine. So, right at the end of the *History*, when Artayctes is awaiting execution, one of his guards was cooking dried fish: the fish suddenly jumped as if it were alive and fresh, and everyone was amazed [*ethaumazon*]. Artayctes commented:

My Athenian friend, do not be afraid of this marvel [*teras*]. It is to me and not to you that Protesilaus of Elaeus reveals this sign – that even though he is dead and dried he has the power, thanks to the gods, to punish the wrongdoer.[42]

Artayctes sees in this wonder a message for himself from the hero Protesilaus, a message about divine retribution. This is a Persian's interpretation of a fish (and enough has already been said about Herodotus' undercutting of the trustworthiness of human accounts). Yet not only is Artayctes about to be punished with death – and last words are inevitably prophetic in Greek tradition from Homer onwards – but also there has been much already in the narrative to suggest that divine retribution is an expectation of Herodotus' understanding of the patterning of events – and this is the final page of the history of the Persian disaster. The story shows Herodotus' characters recognizing the divine as a causal agent, and, while Herodotus offers no direct comment on the accuracy of such a prediction, he has already provided enough in the narrative *both* to doubt *and* to assent to the truth of this perception of theodicy.

---

[42] Her. 9. 120. On the ending of Herodotus, see Boedeker (1988); Herington (1991) and especially Dewald (1997). See Nagy (1990), 269–73 on the wider significance of fish and portents.

This subtle deployent of the divine within the narrative is pervasive in Herodotus. Cyrus asks Croesus why on earth he attacked him, and Croesus, referring to the oracle that if he went to war a great kingdom would fall, replies: 'the god of the Greeks was the cause [aitios] of these things when he encouraged me to war'.[43] Croesus goes on to beg Cyrus to allow him to send to Delphi and to reproach the god by asking if it is customary for him to deceive his benefactors.[44] The Delphic oracle replies first that 'no-one, not even a god, can escape fate', and that by his defeat Croesus has expiated the crime of his ancestor, five generations back, who had murdered his king and master. Secondly, explains the oracle, Croesus should not find fault with Delphi. If it was ambiguous, he should have asked a second question for clarification. 'Let him admit himself responsible [aitios] because he did not comprehend the oracle nor did he ask again'.[45] Croesus concedes that this is fair.

Herodotus previously has shown Croesus testing the oracle at Delphi and finding it right: now the historian has the oracle reveal that on the one hand the crime of Croesus' ancestor demands expiation and, on the other, that Croesus' own misinterpretation is the problem (as if Croesus could have avoided such expiation if he had but asked a follow-up question). What's more, Herodotus is also showing how Croesus' relationship with Delphi has indeed led him to his bitter end. Human dealings with the divine, then, are a constant source of motivation and discussion in Herodotus' *History*.

Herodotus himself as historian also deals directly with the divine. After the battle of Plataea, no Persian bodies were found in the sacred grove of Demeter despite the fighting all around it:

It is a wonder [thôma] that with the fighting around the grove of Demeter not one of the Persians entered the sanctuary or died in it, but very many died around the temple in the unconsecrated area. I judge – if it is necessary to make a judgement in some way about the divine – that the goddess herself did not receive them, since they had burnt her sanctuary at Eleusis.[46]

A wonder provokes a speculation about divine causation, duly marked as a speculation by the qualification clause, 'if it is necessary to make a judgement in some way about the divine'. This comment is not just a piety, but also looks towards contemporary theological thought, epitomized by Protagoras' famously agnostic opening words to his treatise on

---

[43] Her. 1. 87.
[44] Her. 1. 90.
[45] Her. 1. 90.
[46] Her. 9. 65.

the gods: 'concerning the gods I am not in a position to know either what they are or what they are not, or what they look like; for there are many things that prevent knowledge, the obscurity of the matter and the brevity of human life'.[47] Such agnosticism does not prevent Herodotus refusing to tell some stories out of religious scruple, and seeing divine retribution as one pattern in the grand scheme of things. Such expressions are rarely direct, however. Typically, when he sees the earthquake at Delos as a portent [*teras*], sent by a god as a sign of impending evils, he adds *kou*, 'I suppose', 'perhaps'.[48] Like his characters, Herodotus sees god's hand at work in the world; unlike most of his characters, he is capable of dissecting such claims, and of turning an analytic eye on Greek and barbarian religious practices, and he is more than willing to hedge his recognition of divine plotting with hesitation and qualification.

Wonder – *thôma* – and the divine are integrally linked in the *History*'s narrative.[49] It is striking that, unlike Homer, Herodotus very rarely indeed names any particular god as a causal agent, and rarely declares any precise divine intention in events. More often events are said to reveal the influence of *ho theos*, 'god', or *to theion*, 'the divine'. Divine epiphany is both accepted and subjected to sceptical enquiry and radical judgement; 'there are many proofs [*tekmêria*] that there is a divine influence [*ta theia*] on affairs'[50] – and the production of such proof, such evidence, is necessary for the historian. Herodotus provides remarkable testimony to the clash between scientific and theological explanation. The *thôma* which prompts the perception of the divine, like the *thôma* prompted by nature or the social customs of elsewhere, led not to awestruck worship or silent belief, but the enquiry and reflection which make up *historiê*.

IV

We have already seen that Herodotus puts his own name first in the *History* and we have already seen on several occasions how he qualifies his collection of material with commentary about its believability, plausibility and truth. How does Herodotus create an authoritative position for the historian? How does he come to speak with authority

---

[47] This comment is set in context by Kerferd (1981), 163–72.
[48] Her. 6. 98.
[49] Lots of examples in Harrison (2000), 64–101.
[50] Her. 9. 100.

about such a wealth of information and so grand a narrative of warring nations?

Herodotus speaks in passing about his own techniques of composition on several occasions.[51] So, reflecting on the tales of a treacherous liaison between Xerxes, the Persian king, and the city of Argos, he specifies: 'I cannot speak with accuracy, nor am I displaying any opinion on these matters, except what the Argives themselves say . . . I am bound to say what has been said, but I am certainly not bound to believe it all; let this principle hold for all of my argument'.[52] This might make it seem as though Herodotus simply travels around and collects stories (and he has often been taken in this light as a kind of antique folklore buff, compiling traditional tales; so too it has been asked how a historian could preserve stories he knows not to be true – as if the circulation of false or half-true stories does not have a significant motivational force in society or in events). Such a portrayal is hopelessly inadequate both with regard to the specific comment quoted above, and with regard to the *History* in general. For Herodotus' statement of principle here has a specific rhetorical agenda. He is talking of the still highly polemical issue of who collaborated during the war, and he is defending his position on the claims and counterclaims of the Argives by parading his own scrupulous disengagement. The remarks that I excluded from my first quotation of this passage are a generalization, that if everyone put their own faults on the table to swap, everyone would want to keep their own. Herodotus is attempting to avoid the self-serving blame that turned intercity rivalry into violent dispute. It is quite insufficient to read his defensiveness here as a principle of naive reportage.

Nor would the *History* as a whole bear out such a picture. We have already seen the historian carefully dissecting competing claims about the causes of the flooding of the Nile, with logical argument, dismissive scorn and carefully marked speculation. There are many such controversies, often provoking dogmatic dismissiveness ('I laugh when I see many people drawing maps of the world now, and no-one expounding them sensibly'[53]) and often a more careful language of deduction ('I cannot exactly say what language the Pelasgians spoke, but if one must argue from inference . . .'[54]). He also distinguishes between stories he has heard and his own research and opinions ('From my own enquiries,

---

[51] Well collected by Lateiner (1989); Dewald (1987) is a particularly good discussion.
[52] Her. 7. 152–3.
[53] Her. 4. 36.
[54] Her. 1. 57.

I discover . . .'[55]), and dismisses some stories as beyond credibility ('What they say is not convincing to me . . .'[56]), and studs his narrative with repeated indications of his authorial presence ('it seems to me' . . ., 'in my opinion' . . .[57]) – the marks of a personal voice of persuasion and performance.

The voice of the author as a personal, evaluating, reviewing presence is constantly being performed in the *History*. He interweaves his easy narrative style and claims just to tell the stories he hears with his critical arguments and evident intellectual polemic. This means that even the explicit denial of evaluation becomes part of the rhetoric of authorization. The author's refusal to pass judgement becomes a lure for the reader to adopt a critical position, to engage in the process of *historiê*. So the hesitations and qualifications about truth, accuracy and plausibility *buttress* his assertiveness elsewhere. The self-recognized limitations of his knowledge are also devices to frame and support the declarations of fact. Herodotus is deeply concerned with being persuasive – and he knows well that a little uncertainty, a display of carefulness, a withdrawal from arrogant self-assertion, are all part of the weaponry of convincing an audience.

To what, then, does Herodotus elicit assent? What is an audience persuaded to accept? In part, it is a tissue of tales and images of the Mediterranean world (the Greeks and the barbarians); in part, it is an overall view of the Persian war as a tragic overreaching of Persian power, and the remarkable inability of the wealth and luxury of the despot to defeat the hardy resistance of the free. But there are two elements of his narrative persuasiveness which I would like to emphasize and which are less obvious and all the more seductive for being less obvious.

The first concerns motivation – *aitiê*. One of the causes offered for the Persian invasion of Greece is developed in Book III. The Greek doctor Democedes was a prisoner who had successfully cured Darius and now lived in Susa in splendour as an enforced exile from his homeland. He was summoned to treat Atossa, the wife of Darius, who had an abscess on her breast (which had grown and burst because she was too embarrassed to mention it earlier). He agreed to cure it, provided she promised that she would do whatever he asked – though, of course, he would ask for nothing shameful. Consequently, in bed that night Atossa spoke to Darius: 'My Lord, you sit in possession of immense power; but

---

[55] Her. 2. 50.
[56] Her. 5. 86.
[57] Well collected by Lateiner (1989).

you have added neither any kingdom nor power to the Persian empire. It is suitable for someone young and the master of great wealth to make some clear public display so that the Persians will know well that they are ruled by a real man.'[58] Greece should be conquered. And she suggests Democedes as a suitable guide to lead a reconnaissance mission to Greece.

Democedes' motivation is to return home; he uses his medical privilege to make a demand on the queen, whose bed-pillow conversation is reported verbatim by the historian. It would be easy to question what possible access Herodotus could have had to a night-time conversation in the royal bed-chamber. But my point is not to test the historian's veracity here. Rather what interests me here is the nature of the narrative that Herodotus provides. He outlines a set of highly personal and intimate reasons for the grand events that follow. His idea of history is a narrative motivated by individual human decisions, errors, misunderstandings and desires – here dramatized in a dialogue between husband and wife, and prompted by the doctor. Again and again, historical narrative is displayed not as the grand movements of men, economic or social policy, or the changing *Zeitgeist* – but as the behaviour of individuals. This narrative strategy is deeply seductive: the vividness of the details, the engagingly direct persuasiveness of the tale of a man's error, lead the reader through the narrative. But it is still a particular *form* of explanation. The memorability of Herodotus' stories of individual humans, struggling in the world, provides a model for each reader to conceive of him or herself as a historical agent. It's a version of history against which other types of history – economic history, social history, Marxian history – stand out. These charming tales, it should not be forgotten, also project a way of conceptualizing the world and human action in it.

The second form of persuasiveness is related to the easy narrative lure of the first. Consider the celebrated opening story of Gyges and Candaules. Candaules, the king, becomes erotically besotted with his own wife. He wishes to show her off to Gyges, one of his bodyguards. He asks Gyges to stand behind a curtain so that he can view her naked. Gyges is horrified and refuses – until the king's authority forces him to consent. Unluckily, the queen catches a glimpse of him as he slips out of the room from behind the curtain. Gyges is summoned by her, and presented with a choice – either kill the king and marry the queen, or be

---

[58] Her. 3. 134.

put to death: 'Either he must die who made such a plot, or you must die for seeing me naked and thus transgressing the law'.[59] Gyges was amazed [*thôma*] but is persuaded to kill the king and to take up power.

Herodotus tells the story in an enthralling manner. Again, easy though it would be to ask questions about its historical veracity, what is more important is what is conveyed to the audience. Is there not a message about the danger of erotic attraction, especially for a man, especially for a man in power? Is there not a message about how power is transferred in palaces, especially Eastern palaces with their intrigues and marital imbroglios? Is there not a question about a woman's contribution to the pursuit of power, especially a foreign woman? That is, Herodotus' tale depends on – and projects and promotes – a set of ideological assumptions about Eastern power (and Greek tyranny) and about the narrative of revolution in a palace society, and about gender. Stories are powerful tools in the contests of ideology – and Herodotus knows this well and is a brilliantly persuasive writer, especially when his story-telling so well conceals its ability to mould and direct its audience.

Herodotus' prose, then, is not the earliest prose we know of, nor the first work of scientific enquiry. Yet the prime position the ancients awarded Herodotus as the Father of History (and the Father of Lies) is well taken. His prose marks a turning point in the cultural revolution of the classical city. The project of memorializing the great deeds of the past to provide not just a celebration of such grandeur but also a model for the present draws on the epic precedents of Homer and Hesiod, but constructs a quite different image of the world and how to comprehend it. Herodotus' prose projects its author as a critical observer, engaged in the stories he tells, and in the work of persuasion and analysis. The natural world and man's engagement with it require investigation and discussion to be comprehended, as do the multiple stories that circulate. History's watchword now is 'man as the measure of all things' – including the limits of his own comprehension. Herodotus' self-conscious intellectualism also calls the Greek reader to a new sense of his place in things. With the invention of prose comes a new idea of Greekness, which brings also a heightened sense of cultural relativism. In all ways, Herodotus' prose is redrawing the boundaries of the Greek world.

---

[59] Her. 1. 11.

V

Thucydides demands to be read against Herodotus. Although no formal, established genre of 'history' can be said to have yet existed in the fifth century BCE, ancient and modern readers alike have seen Thucydides' *History* of the Peloponnesian War to be in competition with his great predecessor's history of the Persian War. His *History*, he tells us, was written and revised as the events of the war unfurled, and it appears that the work was left unfinished, although it refers to the end of the war, when Thucydides died, probably around 404.[60] Its structure and methodology and narrative set it against Herodotus. Thucydides significantly (if briefly) fills in the story from the end of Herodotus' history to the beginning of the Peloponnesian War; he explicitly rejects the style and the subject matter adopted by Herodotus; and, above all, he establishes both the role of the historical researcher, and what the prose must look like to fulfil that role, in a quite different manner from Herodotus.

Thucydides' opening paragraph shows this competitive self-presentation vividly and with considerable intellectual sophistication. Here is the first sentence:

Thucydides from Athens wrote his account of the war which the Peloponnesians and the Athenians fought against each other, beginning from when the war broke out, because he expected that it would be major and the most worthy of discussion of previous events, judging this from the fact that both sides came to it at the height of their power in all forms of preparation, and recognizing that the rest of Greece was aligned with one side or another, some at that point, though others were still deciding.

Normally, in an English translation, I would want to break this single sentence into more than one sentence (as most modern translations do), but it is worth the inelegance, I think, to keep some sense of the boldness and difficulty of this extraordinary beginning. Let us look at it in some detail. Like Herodotus, Thucydides puts his own name first and gives his city of origin. Thucydides is an Athenian, writing about the war of the Athenians and Peloponnesians: this is to be an insider's account, although this will not be the victor's story, as history is said always to be, since Athens lost the Peloponnesian war. Thucydides' account tells of the collapse of his own city, and a fully tragic sense of a

---

[60] References to the end of the war: Thuc. 2. 65; 5. 26.

great city's self-inflicted disasters informs the narrative.[61] What's more, Thucydides the Athenian not only plays a role as a failed military leader in this war (as he himself recounts), but also is exiled from Athens. A sense of loss veins this history, for all its famed appeals to objectivity.

Where Herodotus presented his research within a model of performance or display, Thucydides presents himself as a *writer*. The verb he uses to describe his work is *xungraphein*, literally, 'to bring together in writing'.[62] This is a prose word in all senses. It does not occur in verse, and from this first charged use on, it becomes almost a technical term for historical composition in prose. It implies a particular contract with the reader. Whether Thucydides' work was ever read aloud to an audience or not, his prose is offered here as a text which is composed for a reader's careful consumption. This agenda is given its most celebrated expression a little later when Thucydides sets out his objectives as a writer. He concludes that his history is conceived as 'a possession for all time, rather than a competitive piece [*agônisma*] for immediate listening'.[63] Thucydides' history is the product of slow and diligent study, and it requires from the reader in turn slow and diligent study, which, he declares, will infinitely repay the effort. It's worth noting, however, that his sniffy dismissal of the instant pleasures of competitive display is competitive enough in itself – and it is striking that Thucydides claims immortality not for marvellous deeds, as Homer and Herodotus did, but for his *own* work. It is *his prose* that is to last for all time.

This primacy of the historian is evident throughout the first sentence, from the proper name on. For what ties Thucydides' sentence together is the historian's activity, stressed in four parallel, linking participles: *arkhomenos*, 'beginning from' – that is, the moment the historian began his work; *elpisas*, 'because he expected that . . .' – that is, the historian's understanding of coming events; *tekhmairomenos*, 'judging this . . .' – that is, his collection and evaluation of evidence; *horôn*, 'recognizing that . . .' – his intellectual comprehension. The historian's intellect dominates the unfurling of this first sentence. Indeed, the historian has evaluated that this is a major war, he insists, not because of promised wonders but because it it is 'most worthy of discussion'. Thucydides avoids Homer's and Herodotus' language of memorial and celebration, however grand the subject: what counts is that this is a work of analysis and discussion: his work. The dim echo of Herodtus in the expression 'which they

[61] See especially Macleod (1983), 140–58; also Moles (1993), 112–13; Finley (1967), 1–55.
[62] See Hornblower (1991b) ad loc.
[63] Thuc. 1. 22.

fought against one another' serves to stress the very different agenda and project.[64]

This densely impressive opening establishes an aggressively intellectual frame for the history, with Thucydides, the historian, at its centre. He continues with an immediate justification (*gar*, 'for') of the declaration that this war is the most worthy of discussion: 'For this was the biggest action [*kinêsis*: 'movement', 'dislocation', a really modern-sounding and abstract word[65]] for the Greeks and a large part of the barbarians – that is to say, the whole world.' And this claim of grandeur is immediately justified (*gar*, 'for') with a further statement of methodological principle – as Thucydides' commitment to serious theoretical reflection is emphasized once more:

> For it was not possible to find out clearly about events which happened before this (and still earlier events) because of the passage of time; but from the evidence available for me to trust, after very long investigation, I do not consider those earlier events to have been major with regard either to war or to other matters.[66]

Thucydides denigrates all previous conflicts, including the Persian War, as insignificant in comparison with his war, but what is really important is the terms in which he does so. The historian has undertaken a 'very long investigation', judging evidence, searching for clarity and certainty, forming a considered opinion. That is what counts. It is hard not to set this passion for scientific analysis against Herodotus' willingness to repeat the tales of the Persian *logioi* in his opening paragraphs (not to mention all the self-attested unbelievable stories in the rest of that history). It is no surprise that modern historians, keen to ground their work in objective analytical principle, have been quick to take Thucydides as the founding father of history. History is declared to be what the historian can prove from an analysis of collected evidence: that is the aim and purpose of this prose.

This, then, is Thucydides' first statement of what is special about his prose. He follows it with a long section known as the 'archaeology', which consists of a sharply speculative account of the past of Greece, based on the theories of contemporary intellectuals.[67] (*Gar*, 'for', it begins: the first five sentences of Thucydides which together take up a whole page of text, are each linked with *gar* as the relentless logic of

---

[64] For the echoes of Herodotus in this opening see e.g. Moles (1993), 99–107.
[65] See the useful note of Connor (1984), 21 n.4.
[66] Thuc. 1. 1.
[67] One of the most discussed (and often reviled) sections of the work: see Hunter (1982), 17–49; Farrar (1988), 138–46; Price (2001), 333–44 (all with further bibliography).

explanation is enforced.) Where Homer saw the past as a time when heroes were stronger, fitter and more beautiful than anyone today, and Hesiod found in the past a Golden Age of perfection, Thucydides sees the past as a time of material and political poverty, with a constant shifting of populations and little action of significance. The Trojan War and even the rise of the Persian empire are briefly covered – all under the rubric of the insurmountable difficulty of writing about such periods without solid evidence. This is a starkly rationalist account which sees political and social change as the result of material conditions and the pursuit of power and wealth (no rapes, no gods, no individual heroism here). Tellingly, the length of the Trojan War is explained not in Homer's grand heroic terms of struggle and resistance, but as the product of the failure of finances and supply lines: 'the cause [*aition*] was not lack of manpower so much as lack of resources' is his brilliantly laconic conclusion.[68] The past comes out in this picture as grim, disjointed and poor: all of which acts as a foil to the first really grand war, which he is about to narrate. This all constitutes a brilliant and harsh rejoinder to Herodotus and Homer and their view of the glories of former years.

This intense, austere, provocative and highly intellectual version of early history ends with a further, quite remarkable methodological statement. 'For most people', he declares, 'searching for the truth is an indifferent activity; they incline to what is simply available'.[69] What's more, the historian's use of evidence is more reliable than 'the poets [*poiêtai*] who decorate and exaggerate in their songs' or the 'chroniclers [*logographoi*] who compose more to attract listeners than to find the truth. Their evidence cannot be tested, and most of it, because of the passage of time, is untrustworthy and passed into myth'.[70] Thucydides powerfully distinguishes his own project from what ordinary people do: this is elite literature, demanding an exclusive audience in its passion for hard truth. He distinguishes himself from poets because they distort and exaggerate the truth (it would be hard to find such a general distinction between poetry and prose before this date, but the accusation of exaggeration and distortion become a commonplace of attacks on poetry over the centuries).[71] But not any prose will do: those who write *logoi*, 'chroniclers', 'speech composers', are also unacceptable. And

---

[68] Thuc. 1. 11.
[69] Thuc. 1. 20.
[70] Thuc. 1. 21.
[71] See Ford (forthcoming); Gould (1990).

the reasons are fascinating. On the one hand, their prose cannot be 'tested' [*anexelenkta*]: that is, they are not subject to *elenchus*, a legal cross-examination. This is the name given to Socratic questioning and is a word easily associated with fifth-century democratic accountability (although certainly not limited to such a political context). Truth needs testing. On the other hand, their desire to attract an audience means that these *logographoi* slip happily into the untrustworthy world of mythic tales.[72] (Tellingly, the divine, so often a battleground between myth and history, makes an appearance in Thucydides, unlike Herodotus, only as evidence of humans' misunderstandings and foolish desperation.) Historical prose is here fighting for its place in the multiplying genres of writing the past. It does so by claiming a privileged relationship to truth – how truth should be sought and tested. Thucydides is asserting the intellectual primacy of his prose technique.

There is more. Thucydides goes on to underline two further principles of his composition. The first concerns speeches. He has included in his history the great speeches that were delivered before and during the war, he explains, but 'I have found it hard to remember the exact wording of those I heard, as have my informants from various places. Consequently, while I have kept as closely as possible to the general sense of what was truly said, I have said what in my opinion was demanded by the circumstances'.[73] There is no way to reconcile the contradictory ideas in this remark. If the speaker said what the circumstances required in Thucydides' opinion, then the remark has no purchase. If the speaker did *not* say what the situation needed, then Thucydides cannot stay as closely as possible to what was truly said. The passion for accuracy and testing here is in marked tension with the desire for a narrative which reveals what is necessary or suitable [*ta deonta*]. We will see shortly how this tension is worked through in the body of the *History*.

The second principle is a commitment to evaluation and accuracy – which is also expressed with considerable complexity. 'I have made it a principle not to write down what I learnt immediately, nor what seemed to me to be the case, but in events I was present at or learnt about from others, I have gone through each with as much precision as possible.'[74]

---

[72] On History's rejection of Myth, see Detienne (1986) (although this translation is particularly poor), Cartledge (1993), 18–35 (with useful bibliography). Thomas (1989), Lloyd (1979) and Vernant (1983) are crucial background reading here.

[73] Thuc. 1. 22.

[74] Thuc. 1. 22.

Herodotus wrote down the stories he heard, he says, and readily adds 'it seems to me' at points through his narrative. Thucydides, however, requires accuracy [*akribeia*] even when he was present at events.[75] This commitment to critical evaluation, however, has a wider purpose. History for Thucydides should aim to be *useful* [*khrêsimon*]. Because of human nature [*to anthrôpinon*], similar events will happen again, and Thucydides' analyses will prove a (critical, accurate) guide. Thucydides' history contains a message about what it is to be human, a human engaged in the struggle for power and authority. History, for Thucydides, is important because of what it can show of the general and the abstract. It is this promise to reveal the pattern of 'the human'[76] which makes his history, he concludes, 'a possession for all time'.[77]

Thucydides ends his introduction with a summary statement of a general cause for why the war started, which he calls 'the most true reason, though one concealed'[78] by explicit arguments about causes. This underlying cause is 'the growth of Athenian power and the fear it produced in the Spartans'.[79] Thucydides aims to uncover what would otherwise be unrecognized: it is not marvellous deeds that are to lead the reader on but the seduction of an analytic insight into the real truth of things. And with that, twenty-three chapters and many pages in, Thucydides begins his narrative of the war . . .

These opening pages of Thucydides are remarkably difficult. The language is tough. It is syntactically intricate, even rebarbative; its vocabulary is abstract and powerfully novel. Conceptually, it is densely argued and often obscure. It is fierce writing. And that is part of the point. Its claim to be a new and privileged form of expression, a new accounting, is *performed* in every sentence: it lures by its very difficulty, by its promise of a special understanding. Above all, it demands not just a different comprehension of the past of Greece and the narrative of war but also a different concept of reader and text. Thucydides rejects the seductions of easy listening in favour of hard work, careful collection and sifting of evidence, and precise evaluation – which in turn requires a

---

[75] On *akribeia*, see Crane (1996), 32–8 and 50–74.

[76] See e.g. Cogan (1981) on this.

[77] Thuc. 1. 22.

[78] Thuc. 1. 23: for a useful summary of the arguments about this phrase see Hornblower (1991b), 64–6.

[79] Thuc. 1. 23. de Ste. Croix (1972) discusses Thucydides' case most fully, though not wholly convincingly; Orwin (1994), 30–63. The contrast between superficial and profound causes has been called 'Thucydides' greatest single contribution to later history-writing' (Hornblower [1991b], 65). On the idea of *prophasis*, see Rawlings (1975), though his conclusions on this passage are unnuanced.

new form of attention from its readers. To read Thucydides inevitably means being drawn into his world of testing, abstract conceptualization – his intellectualized, passionately analytical view of cause and action. His prose redraws the intellectual map of Greece.

VI

The following sections of this chapter look briefly at two of the areas emphasized in Thucydides' introduction, first the use of speeches in his narrative; and second the construction of the authority of the historian.

There is a string of speeches in Thucydides, which appear more formally constructed than Herodotus' rather brief dialogues. This is mainly because Thucydides' speeches are most often dramatic reconstructions of formal proceedings. There are political speeches from the Assembly, debates about policy, a funeral speech over the war dead, a general's words to his troops before battle. Thucydides may not write history as a performance piece [*agônisma*], but he repeatedly stages such competitive displays of oratory for the evaluative appreciation of his readers.

The use of speeches in history – though copied by so many later ancient writers – has caused some critical worry.[80] Why are only these speeches included? The Funeral Speech delivered by Pericles in Book II, for instance, is the only funeral speech presented, although the institution was an annual event. Sometimes, only one speech – one side – of a debate is offered. When Athens voted first to destroy the city of Mytilene which had revolted against the Athenian Empire, and then voted later to rescind the first vote, only two speeches, both from the second debate, are reported. What is to be made of the fact that Thucydides allows himself such creative licence in what he presents as the *ipsissima verba* of the leading figures of his narrative? When Pericles' speech to the Athenian Assembly (1.140) seems to answer point by point the speech of the Corinthian ambassadors to a Spartan Assembly (1.120ff.), has the attraction of dramatic effect outweighed plausible accuracy?

Now, speech-making is a central element of the political life of Athens

---

[80] See Stadter ed. (1973) with bibliography of earlier discussions; Hornblower (1987), 45–72; Cogan (1981), and especially Macleod (1983) which remains seminal. The best study of a single speech in context is Loraux (1986).

and of the diplomacy that runs throughout the war, but the representation of selected speeches allows Thucydides to stage vividly the interplay
of explicit and concealed motivation that his introduction had high-
lighted. We are led to see the force of rhetoric in action in the state. This
is especially emphatic when Thucydides offers his brief analytic commentary to point up the differences and confusions that underlie the
decisions of the citizen body. The debate that results in the Sicilian
expedition demonstrates this wonderfully well.[81] The Athenians have
voted to send 60 ships to Sicily under the command of Alcibiades,
Nicias, and Lamachus. Nicias, says Thucydides, did not wish the
command, because he thought the decision a mistake based on a
specious pretext, and believed that the expedition was too major an
undertaking.[82] The speech he delivers is thus set up as an act designed to
persuade the Athenians to rescind their vote. (We know what he is trying
to achieve.) It is within this light that we should read his attack on
Alcibiades, his fellow general – who, Nicias argues, is too self-satisfied
with his power, as a young man would be. Nicias attacks Alcibiades for
misleading the young men and begs the more experienced citizens 'not
to behave like them, and not to conceive false passion for what is not
there'.[83] Thucydides has Nicias try to expose the 'false passions' of his
opponent, but fail to change his audience's attitude, whose passions he
cannot turn.

The historian then gives Alcibiades' winning reply.[84] He introduces it
with a similar uncovering of a complex context.[85] Alcibiades, he states,
differs in political outlook from Nicias, and had just been personally
attacked in public by him: but his strongest desire was to be a general
and to win honour and wealth for himself. This directs his policy.
Thucydides adds a nuanced, sinuous character portrait: Alcibiades was
a celebrity in the city, but many people feared him because of the
degeneracy of his physical life and the arrogance of his attitude (which
his enemies saw as aiming at tyranny). Yet despite the fact that his
personal life made him objectionable, he was excellent in the manage-
ment of the war for the state. The consequence of the people's fear and
distaste was that 'they entrusted affairs to others, and thus before long
ruined the city'.[86] The icy pragmatism of this conclusion caps the
extraordinary introduction to Alcibiades' speech. It says: listen to the

---

[81] See Cogan (1981), 94–100; Orwin (1994), 118–41; Rood (1998), 162–7; and especially
Macleod (1983), 68–87 and Ober (1994).
[82] Thuc. 6. 8.   [83] Thuc. 6. 12–13.   [84] Thuc. 6. 16–18.
[85] Thuc. 6. 15.   [86] Thuc. 6. 15.

words of the distasteful degenerate who lusts for personal power, but who, if you don't trust him, will let you destroy your own city. Thucydides catches the complex ambivalence of this historical moment – and turns it on his readers with a powerful and bitter edge. Can you evaluate the best route through this morass of dangerous motivation and manipulative power plays? The reader is encouraged to act as if in the audience – to play the judging citizen – and participate again through reading in the debate that led to Athenian destruction. What can – should – you make of Alcibiades' performance?

Revealing in this way the intricate and dramatic interplay of motivation and emotion in the decision-making of the city at war is one of the most powerful effects of Thucydides' representation of speeches, an effect which engages the reader in the passion of close reading of political motivation, its claims and counterclaims. With such speeches, the reader, like the audience in the theatre, watches rhetoric in action, and is encouraged to judge its effects and consequences.

The representation of political speeches is also the technique by which Thucydides shows ideology at work and reveals the character of his leading players. The Mytilenean debate's first speaker is Cleon, who is introduced with a typically snide and pithy comment by Thucydides: 'Cleon had triumphed in the previous debate with its proposal of the death penalty [for all the males of Mytilene]: he was both the most violent of the citizens and the most persuasive among people at that time'.[87] We are thus encouraged to read his speech as a sign of his violent and persuasive character. What he says, however, also offers an insightful display of how the political principles of democracy could be deployed and manipulated in Athenian debate.[88] For in this speech Cleon bases his argument on the nature of democratic power itself and attacks the Athenians for their behaviour in political debate.

'I for my part have often recognized that democracy is incapable of ruling others . . .', he begins.[89] For the Athenians, unused to fear and suspicion in their daily dealings, are easily persuaded into compassion by the speeches of others, and do not realize the true nature of their power, namely, that 'your empire is a tyranny over rebellious and unwilling subjects . . . and you rule depends on superior strength not on your subjects' good feelings towards you'.[90] Tyranny is the anathema

---

[87] Thuc. 3. 36.
[88] For democratic dissent see the fine study of Ober (1998); also Yunis (1996).
[89] Thuc. 3. 37.
[90] Thuc. 3. 37.

of democracy, its despised opposite. But Cleon shockingly calls the democratic empire a tyranny – a term which brings with it awful expectations of violence, fear and suspicion. Democracy has to be prepared to use its force. What's more, there is nothing worse for the city, he continues, than when some intellectuals think themselves better than the laws and try to change them: it is better to keep to the democratic principle that ordinary people know best. The implication is that anyone who tries to change the decision of the first meeting is not acting in a democratic spirit and is probably a dangerous intellectual (rather than a man of the people). Again, the values of democracy are slyly worked in favour of Cleon's own position. He even accuses the citizens of behaving like the audience of a superstar lecturer or in the theatre – just listening and taking pleasure – rather than acting like the political decision-makers they should be:

You are simply victims of your own pleasure in listening and sit like the audience at a sophist show rather than as citizens deliberating about the state.[91]

This is a highly sophisticated and cynical representation. Thucydides has the demagogue talk about the dangers of demagoguery. Rather than political debate – says the politician debating the point – there is here just a display of competitive speech-making. Listening with passive pleasure means a failure of the ideals of active participation in government. The brilliantly sophistic rhetorician, Cleon, thus dismissively scorns the tools of rhetoric – as the ideals of democracy become a twisted token in his violently persuasive argument. Yet Thucydides himself in his introduction had also warned against mere pleasure in listening. Now he seems to require from his readers a critical evaluation of the demagogue's demand for careful listening, as it becomes attached to Cleon's murderous political agenda.

In Cleon's speech, then, we can see how Thucydides shows the sly violence of persuasion at work, and, in particular, the twisting of democratic language in the mouth of the master-demagogue. Thucydides gives only the barest indication of *how* to read the speech in his introductory character sketch of Cleon – but gives enough to make sure we shiver at the irony of Cleon himself arguing for a proper democrat's attention for his proposals. The reader of Thucydides' history – like the audience in the Assembly – has to do his (or her) own judging. Speeches

---

[91] Thuc. 3. 38.

work to engage the reader in the political and ethical issues of the *History*.

The placement of speeches is also a fundamental element in Thucydides' narrative technique. The most famous speech of all is Pericles' Funeral Speech, which sums up what the leading statesman of Athens sees as the true character and greatness of Athens. It is a speech inevitably cited in discussions of Athenian ideology in the classical period.[92] It is not by chance, however, that it comes where it does in the *History*. It is set in Book II after the preliminary drawing up of motives and battlelines for conflict. It is the end of the first year of the Peloponnesian War. It acts first as a summary of Athenian self-representation as a power in the Mediterranean – and, for Thucydides, the growth of Athenian power and the reactions it prompts are the most important cause of the war. Second, the speech expresses, at the beginning of the war, the ideals of Athenian greatness: these ideals will be a contributory factor in Athens' own self-inflicted downfall. It is the fullest statement of the basis of Athenian greatness and tragedy. As in many Greek tragedies, the expression of pride comes before the fall. Thus, thirdly, this speech is followed by the plague which ravages the city (and its ideals) – which heads the long narrative leading to the disasters of the Sicilian expedition. Thucydides uses the Funeral Speech to express in the most glittering terms the glory – the self-glorying – of Athens. Those are the heights from which Athens stumbled into defeat.

The speeches of Thucydides' *History* represent the cut and thrust of competitive display which he rejects as a principle for his own writing. Through these dramatized set pieces of rhetoric, he stages the functioning of ideological posturing, hidden motivation, and dangerous persuasiveness, in Athens' defeat. He engages the reader in the work of analysis, judgement and reflection. Thucydides may wish to exclude himself from the arena of competitive performance, but he certainly sees speech-making as a central element of political life, and brilliantly deploys the seductions and powers of rhetorical performance as a fundamental factor in his history.

---

[92] Bibliography – largely German – in Rusten (1989) ad loc., and Hornblower (1991b) ad loc. See also Connor (1984), 63–78; Ober (1998), 83–9.

VII

Thucydides changes the scope of prose and the understanding of the relation between the author, his material and the reader. I have been focusing on the self-presentation of the historian in the introduction, and on the self-conscious device of dramatizing great speeches of great characters in his *History* – the narrative technique where Thucydides exposes most strongly the possible fissures between the desire for factual reportage and the desire for an explanation of the emotions and complexities of reasoning that make up *to anthrôpinon*, 'what it is to be human'. Yet if there is a single technique that has contributed most effectively to the construction of the author's authority, it is the prose style of his narrative history which enacts those paraded principles of accurate reportage and critically judged evidence.

Thucydides rarely enters his own prose as an explicit commentator – for all that his intellectual, sardonic presence is felt throughout.[93] Although he appears as a character in the third person in the military history of the city, and although he comments explicitly that he was, for example, in Athens during the plague and suffered from it himself, the general tone of the historical narrative is of scrupulous objectivity, and the accumulation of relentlessly precise detail. Numbers – of soldiers, of miles between towns, of dead, of money – are listed. Marches, expeditions, are given their routes and logistics, votes are recorded. Here is a single sentence, which is chosen because it is exemplary of this drive for factuality:

At the beginning of the following summer, the Chians were asking for ships to be sent immediately, and were afraid that the Athenians would see what was being done (for their negotiations had been secret); consequently, the Spartans sent three men of Spartiate rank to Corinth to have the ships transported as quickly as possible from the other side of the Isthmus to face Athens, and to order the whole fleet to sail to Chios including the ships Agis was preparing against Lesbos; the total number of the ships was thirty-nine.[94]

A huge sentence – nearly 90 words in Greek – but clear and direct enough. The time reference and geographical markers locate the action precisely. The movement of forces is itemized both in terms of the motivation of the Chians and the Spartans, and in terms of the precise

---

[93] For good introduction to this issue, with bibliography, see Ober (1998), 52–63.
[94] Thuc. 8. 7.

mission of the fleet of Agis. The messengers who enforce the order are numbered and their social class is given. The final total of the fleet is precise. The sequence of action is coherent and logically explained. And all of this detail is but one preparatory sentence in a far longer account – and little of it will be of consummate importance (or even mentioned) again.

It is this obsessional detailing, the constant accounting, that produces the 'reality effect' – the historian's authoritative representation of the war's action. It must never be forgotten that the most persuasive rhetorical device in Thucydides' armoury of narrative techniques is the direct expression of uncontested and enumerated fact. This empiricism is one voice in Thucydides' texts. The selection and juxtaposition of such facts constructs his argument; the combination of such evidence with his authorial commentary and with the set-piece speeches, together makes Thucydides' *History* the powerfully persuasive work it is. But the deliberately restricted, apparently neutral expression of evidence – 'the total number of the ships of the allies was thirty-nine' – is the bedrock of persuasiveness on which Thucydides' work is laboriously built. It is a technique which prose makes its special province, and which becomes integral to science and philosophy. The power of prose stems from its ability to make its own rhetorical strategies seem natural and transparent. The authority of 'the bare statement of fact' is the most brilliant rhetorical invention of prose.

VIII

The writings of Herodotus and Thucydides found the genre of history – and after them history – rather than epic, say, or mythic genealogy – becomes the privileged model of relating the past. How the past is related determines the present ('If you do not know what happened before you were born', writes Cicero, 'you are destined to spend your life as a child'). The stories of the past are indeed a fundamental element of the formation of an identity. The prose of Herodotus and Thucydides changes the way that the past and a relation to the past are conceptualized: from the first word of their projects, the focus is on a human ability to explain, explore and discuss the past, and this focus requires from the reader an evaluative, engaged critical eye, that is itself a particular way of viewing the world. It is not by chance that the invention of historical prose (with its special critical contract between author and reader) takes place as democracy (with its culture of public judgement and personal responsibility) comes into being. The invention of historical prose is part and parcel of the cultural revolution of the classical city. Herodotus and Thucydides do not just provide powerful narratives of the wars which are integral to Greek ideas of what it means to be Greek or Athenian, they also construct the categories by which experience can be calibrated and articulated – the images and narratives by which we live. Herodotus and Thucydides make historians of us all.

III. RHETORIC: THE AUTHORITY OF SELF-PRESENTATION

'Democracy is a constitution of speech-making', wrote Demosthenes, the great orator of the fourth century.[1] The Assembly is the arena where policy decisions of the state were publicly debated and decided – and where political careers were made and lost. The law courts were a forum not just for conflict resolution but for competition in status between elite males. The theatre staged debate for an audience's reflection. Even in the more private sphere of the *symposium* amid the wine, women and song we see the party game of speeches on a particular topic. In the *agora*, the market place, and, more formally, in the theatre, visiting intellectuals and professional speech-makers – often called 'sophists' – gave speeches for the edification and amusement of a paying audience.[2] What is perhaps as important as this institutional framework is the ideological underpinning of such practices. That both sides of a question must be publicly debated is a constant watchword of democratic principle. That all citizens are equal before the law, and that the provision of a law court with a public jury is basic to a democratic polity – these are principles uncontested in democratic theory. *Isêgoria* – the right of all citizens to speak – is announced in the opening ritual of each Assembly with the herald's question, 'Who wants to speak?'. There is a wonderful phrase that sums up these principles: *es meson*. It means literally 'into the middle' – but implies that a grounding ideal of democracy is that all issues should be set out in public for debate and decision.[3] Demosthenes was right: Athenian democracy can be summed up as a 'constitution of speech-making'.

This institutional and ideological framework makes Athens in the classical era a heady world for the practice and study of rhetoric. Where the routes to power, influence and status so depend on public self-presentation in formal contexts of speech-making, there is a huge premium both on the ability to speak well – and on the ability to teach speaking well. It is in the classical *polis* – and not just Athens, of course –

[1] *En logois politeia*, Dem. 19. 184.
[2] See on performance and participation e.g. Goldhill (1999), 1–32; Sinclair (1988); Ober (1989).
[3] See Vernant (1982); Finley (1983); Loraux (1986); Farrar (1988); Meier (1990); Boegehold and Scafuro edd. (1994).

that language itself becomes an object of intensive study for the first time, and, above all, that the science of rhetoric is constituted as a discipline in its own right.[4] The influence of this invention is felt throughout Greek literature – and indeed throughout the writing of the Western tradition. Rhetoric remained central to education in Western society until quite recently – though some would say that the revitalization of rhetoric in literary criticism (or even in media studies) shows that the resistance to studying rhetoric on the part of the twentieth century was a temporary and misplaced silencing. In the classical *polis*, for the first time there were handbooks (*technai*) that offer to describe and to teach the power of persuasion – culminating in Aristotle's *Rhetoric*. We also have the speeches of the orators who became paradigms of political power through persuasiveness, along with the courtroom speeches of the experts in legal arguments. What's more, we have the set-piece display pieces of the masters of performance of argument. This dazzling combination of the growth of a technical field of study and the masterpieces of its practice form the subject of this chapter.

The power, wealth and opportunities offered by the capital of empire led many intellectuals and performers to Athens from around the Mediterranean. These figures are often known generically as 'the sophists'.[5] Plato in his defence of Socrates, his master, and of philosophy, his discipline, made stinging assaults on 'sophists' and 'sophistry' – sneering at sophists for teaching for pay, for teaching verbal trickery rather than the truth, for promising to teach virtue – but providing merely formulae for easy living. Hence the modern, wholly negative associations of the terms 'sophist' and 'sophistry', which always imply a tricksy and self-interested persuasiveness. Plato was not alone in making such attacks. Aristophanes, the comic playwright, especially in the *Clouds*, pokes fun – to the point of physical violence – at sophists, led by Socrates (to Plato's chagrin). The science of the sophists was sufficiently part of public life to be made into the plot line of a comedy to be performed in front of the whole city, and sufficiently trendy and worrying to be ridiculed. Rhetoric indeed proved a frightening technology, especially to the conservative elements in Athens, which needed to control the sophists with scorn and rejection in direct proportion to their perceived attractiveness and success. The fear of rhetoric is not surprising. In a celebrated slogan,

[4] Kennedy (1963); Swearingen (1991); Cole (1991); Poulakos ed. (1993).
[5] Useful accounts in Kerferd (1981); Guthrie (1962–1981) vol. III; Goldhill (1986), 222–43; de Romilly (1992); and, more polemically, Jarratt (1991); Poulakos (1995).

Protagoras offered 'to make the weaker argument the stronger'. In state policy-making, such skills could lead to military and political disaster. In the courtroom, it could lead to outraged victims, whose rightful cases would lose out to the clever speaker. In the informal exchanges of the city, the trust and reciprocity of social life could break down into suspicion and mistreatment. The threat of rhetoric is a threat to the working of language – to the very basis of the constitution of democracy, as Demosthenes would have it.

The threat of rhetoric is clear enough, then. But so too is its lure. The study of rhetoric promised not corruption, of course, but an essential support for public life; the ability to get your points across forcefully and well; the skill to avoid an enemy's plots; an intellectual control over the vicissitudes of the city of words. The teachers of rhetoric, what's more, taught far more besides: political virtue, literary criticism, mathematics. It was because the sophists had such varied interests and such authority that Plato attacks them so consistently.

One legacy of Plato is the tendency to see the different intellectual figures as forming a group – 'the sophists' – who shared an agenda, as it were, and were recognized and disliked as a group. This is a distorting rhetorical device, however, that conceals a far more interesting reality. First, sophists had a wide range of practices and interests which do not necessarily overlap: medicine, mathematics, linguistics, political theory and so forth.[6] Second, they came from many different backgrounds. Gorgias was an ambassador from Leontini when he first came to speak at Athens. Hippodamus was a political theorist who was responsible for the grid plan of the streets of the Piraeus, the port of Athens. Protagoras drew up the laws for the new city of Thurii. Third, as these last examples show, there were many of these figures who held positions of great authority and respect in their own communities and in Athens – in a way quite lost in the modern usage of the term 'sophist'. Fourth, 'sophist' is too rigid a term. Euripides, the tragedian, shares many interests with 'the sophists'. Critias was a man who could be called a sophist – but he also wrote tragedies, and was one of the tyrants who ruled over Athens in a violent but brief coup at the end of the fifth century. The intellectual interests and political ideas of the leading writers known as the sophists – Protagoras, Hippias, Gorgias and so on – are widely shared and widely debated concerns of the culture of Athens in the fifth and fourth centuries.

[6] See e.g. Lloyd (1987).

It would be better to think of the sophists as trendy and influential intellectual superstars – and to think of their various concerns as different strands of what I have been calling the cultural revolution of Athens. That said, there are types of argument which become so widespread throughout the prose (and verse) writing of the fifth and fourth centuries, that they become key identificatory gestures of the new ways of thinking. Here are four especially marked signs of this 'sophistic thought'.

First, the turn to *nomos* and *phusis*, convention/law and nature, as explanatory categories. We have already seen how the Hippocratic treatise *Airs, Waters, Places* investigated the natural world as an exploration of social and cultural norms of different communities. And we have seen how Herodotus constantly uses the variety of *nomoi* to explore what Greekness itself is, while displaying the wonders of *phusis* – and how Thucydides defines his whole history as the project of revealing human nature, 'the human', as a guide for future generations. The dissemination of this polarity as a form of explanation could also be demonstrated from tragedy, from medicine, from rhetoric. There are two related points I need to make about these keywords of the fifth-century enlightenment. On the one hand, the opposition of 'nature' and 'culture' is iself a sign and a symptom of the rapid cultural change of the classical city. What once seemed natural can now be seen as (merely) conventional; our parents' ways are not our ways; our children do not do what seems obviously proper for us. The contest over what is natural (proper, right) and conventional (arbitrary, open to change, debatable) marks the conflict and worry of social change – in a way which is all too familiar from rapidly changing modern society also.[7] On the other hand, this opposition is really important for the development of history, medicine, philosophy as disciplines to explain the world. For the turn to *nomos* and *phusis* as explanations repeatedly seeks to understand specific events, attitudes, projects as signs of abstract and general principles – which is one of the foundational strategies of science, philosophy and the other self-reflexive disciplines. The decision to punish a city by killing its males is justified now because it is *natural* for power to be exercised by the powerful. The bizarreness of an Indian eating the body of his dead father is explained as a mere difference in *custom*. The general, abstract principles explain, organize and control the variety of the world: a master narrative.

---

[7] See e.g. Bourdieu (1977).

The opposition of *phusis* and *nomos* is thus both a symptom of cultural dislocation and a way of negotiating one's path through the confusion of such cultural change. Whenever someone says 'it's natural that . . .', 'it's conventional that . . .', it indicates a potential argument about what is normal and an attempt to control the situation.

The recognition that different communities have different *nomoi* also combines with the idea that 'man is the measure of all things' to form what is often called 'sophistic relativism'.[8] Not only do different societies have different ways of doing things (which each thinks natural and proper) but also different people have different perceptions (which each think correct and suitable). So a wind may feel cold to one person and hot to another. These contrasting impressions are each valid for the person who feels them. Such an argument may appear to have a rather abstract epistemological aspect – until it is applied to moral values. Can what seems right to any individual be similarly valid? Can justice or morality have a more general application? What are the implications for society if such principles are merely arbitrary and open to personal judgement? There is a slide from a philosophical worry about perception to a conservative nightmare of a moral chaos where any behaviour can be justified: 'what is wrong, if it does not seem so to the person doing it?', as a character in Euripides asks.[9] The association of sophistic argumentation with a collapse of social order feeds the fear of rhetoric's power.

The second sign of sophistic thinking is what can be called 'the argument from probability'. The standard Greek word here is *eikos*, 'probable', 'likely', 'reasonable', 'usual'. One of the first lessons of the rhetorical handbooks is that if you want to be convincing to a jury, you should not state directly what you think is the truth, but rather you should always construct your argument from likelihood. So our earliest rhetorical handbooks, we are told, set up a case. A fight has broken out between a large man and a small man, and the question is who started it. The small man is instructed to argue 'Is it likely that I, a small man, would pick a fight with a large man, when it is obvious that I would be beaten up?'. The large man is instructed to argue 'Is it likely that I, a large man, would pick a fight with a small man when it is obvious that the blame would fall on me?'.[10] In both cases, saying simply 'He started

---

[8]   As discussed by Kerferd (1981), 83–110, and in more technical detail by e.g. Sinclair (1976); Burnyeat (1976); Schiappa (1991).

[9]   Eur. fr. 19 (from the *Aiolos*).

[10]   The exact source of these arguments – reported by Aristotle *Rhet.* 1402a17 and Plato *Phaedrus* 273a–b – is debated. It is attributed rather vaguely to Corax or Tisias; but in either case functions as an exemplary case of the argument from probability.

it', or 'I didn't do it' is seen as unconvincing, even if true. This example may seem trivial. But not only is this type of argument central to speeches of political deliberation and legal wrangling throughout the classical era, but also the dangerous fear of rhetoric can be sensed here strongly. If, when you are innocent, it is no longer enough to say 'I am innocent, I didn't do it', the corollary of rhetoric's training is the failure of the simple statement of fact – which releases the deep-seated anxiety that language can be a trap in which you can be manipulated and humiliated.

Aristotle has the most extended formal discussion of this type of argument. For Aristotle, *to eikos* ('likelihood', 'the usual') develops a very strongly normative sense – not merely what is likely, but also what is generally the case, and thus normal. He sees the appeal to the normal as an essential tool of rhetoric and he calls this argument the 'enthymeme'.[11] By this he means an argument that depends not on formal logic so much as on the deployment of the stereotypes of the normal. The enthymeme is an argument that takes as its premise a generally accepted but not stated view of its audience. It aims to win over its audience by getting inevitable agreement for the premise, on which the speaker then builds his case. Such arguments may have the form of a logical case ('if/since x, then y'): 'since all politicians wish to hold on to power, we must expect this man's policies to be aimed at pleasing the voters'. Or the stereotype can be included in an apparent statement or question: 'Would an intelligent woman go to such a place dressed in such a manner?' Aristotle lists a large number of types of enthymeme – all of which appeal to and manipulate the 'likely' or the 'probable' as their basis.

It is fascinating to trace this development in theoretical understanding, from our first extant instructional manual or treatise, the *Dissoi Logoi* ('Twinned' or 'Double Arguments'),[12] through the performed speeches of law court and Assembly, to the extended and systematized philosophical discussion of Aristotle. This sort of development is integral to the field of rhetoric, and shows well the dynamic interrelations between theory and practice constantly at work.

The third strategy of sophistic thought could be summed up under the heading 'reversal and paradox'. As the title *Dissoi Logoi* suggests, and as the law court and Assembly institutionalize, 'two sides to each

---

[11] For a heavy-duty philosophical account of the enthymeme, see Burnyeat (1994) and (1996).
[12] This bizarre piece is usefully edited and translated in Robinson (1979).

question' is a principle both of democracy and of the new intellectuals. But sophistic rhetoricians revel in the ability to turn arguments upside down and to construct wilful paradoxes. Socrates' most famous ideas are both such paradoxes: 'no-one does wrong willingly', and 'I am wise only in that I know I know nothing'. In both cases, Plato constructs lengthy arguments to justify these positions: but in both cases it is the shock of the apparently outrageous claim which is the starting point, the hook for his audience's engagement.[13] Shortly, I will be looking at Gorgias' *Encomium to Helen*, a speech which praises and exonerates the adulteress from blame. It is typical of his sophistic flair to take the indefensible – that a woman who commits adultery should be praised – and write a brilliant performance on the subject.

Plato often trivializes such arguments as mere word-mongering, and Aristophanes imagines a hilarious debate between 'Just Argument' and 'Unjust Argument' in the *Clouds* (which 'Unjust Argument' wins with increasingly vulgar and uproarious manipulation); Aristophanes also has a son argue that it is right for him to beat his own father. But the *threat* of rhetoric is again evident for all the joking and scorn. 'To make the weaker argument the stronger' – itself an outrageous claim – makes the link between language and power in the state a source of contention and concern. From Thucydides' speeches, to Demosthenes' political tirades, to Aristotle's theorizing, the power of argument to effect the business of the city is a source of passionate concern and regulation.

The fourth area of sophistic thought I wish to stress again links rhetoric, power and social change, and this is the broad subject of 'teaching virtue' – including good character, political expertise, ethical action, military expertise. Whether virtue, conceived that broadly, can be taught is one of the obsessively debated questions of the period. Who the best teachers for a young man are, what subjects he should learn, and even the abstract issue of whether any teaching is possible in such an area, are all questions repeatedly brought into the public eye. Many of Plato's dialogues in particular reflect the broad nature of this debate. In the *Laches*, Socrates meets two great generals, Laches and Nicias, at a performance of military skill by a heavily armed warrior, and a discussion develops as to why the generals' children are not great men like their parents, and what form of teaching they should seek to better them. The *Ion* sets Socrates against a rather dim bard, Ion, who claims that knowing Homer is all anyone needs by way of education. In the

---

[13] See Vlastos (1991); Kahn (1995).

Meno, Socrates – to make a point about the theory of knowledge – teaches a slave geometry. Whether Gorgias and Protagoras really teach excellence forms part of the critique in the dialogues *Protagoras* and *Gorgias*. Plato, of course, has his particular agenda in that he wants to make philosophy *the* dominant model of education, but his image of the Athenians from general to slave debating education in this way finds support in the array of other texts and arenas where such questions also arise.

Now, what makes a citizen a good citizen is, in general terms, inevitably a political issue. But there is a more precise set of political concerns which makes education such a hot topic in the classical *polis*. First, if we look back to the archaic period, we will find that a poet like Theognis advises young men 'to spend time with the good/noble [*esthlos*], if you wish to be good/noble [*esthlos*]'.[14] That is, excellence, the possession of the best men, is passed on in birth and breeding on the one hand, and in the correct environment of a noble life on the other. Excellence is an exclusive and excluding idea – aristocratic rule depends on holding on to what is 'best' [*ariston*]. So in Homer's poetry the focus of its narrative of excellence is almost exclusively on the great princes of the Greek world, and when the action shifts to the less exalted world of the farms on Ithaca in the *Odyssey*, the excellence of the lower-level figures consists in knowing their place and working to maintain the hierarchy of the palace (and the swineherd Eumaeus who is instrumental in saving his master, Odysseus, is said to have been born the son of a king).[15] Yet the sophists offered to teach anyone who could pay, and democracy provided a stage – in theory at least – on which any citizen could excel. The new education offered new access to power. The new knowledege offered non-aristocratic citizens the opportunity to rise in status and authority – which could seem to aristocratic forces a recipe for social chaos. (The parallels with contemporary society do not need expounding.) Hence, the political *frisson* around teaching excellence.

This political charge is most strikingly seen in the case of Socrates. Socrates was put to death on charges of introducing new gods and of corrupting the young. Although it is difficult to trace the ins and outs of how this trial came about and what Socrates may have said in it, it seems extremely likely that the charge of corrupting the young came about because of Socrates' association as a teacher with some extremely

---

[14] Theognis 35–8: see Figueira and Nagy edd. (1985).
[15] *Od.* 390–484; on class in the *Odyssey* see Rose (1992), 92–140.

dangerous political characters.[16] Socrates was perceived to be the leading intellectual star in the circle which included Alcibiades, whose treachery led to the defeat of Athens in the Peloponnesian War, and Critias, the leading tyrant in the violent and bloody oligarchic coup that so racked the city. What makes a citizen good – or bad – here becomes a burning issue. The polemical role education plays in the violent history of Athens is what the charge against Socrates highlights.

I have offered these four signposts to sophistic thought partly because these models of expression become so prevalent in the texts of the classical *polis*: this broad dissemination underlines how such rhetoric becomes an integral expectation of exchange in this period, and cannot be limited to a defined group called 'the sophists'. But my aim has also been to emphasize how each of these argumentative strategies has a political dimension and is seen to contribute broadly to the social conflicts of the period. Whether it is a general worry about social chaos in the rapidly changing city, or a fear of losing a court case unfairly, or a concern that the youth of the city are being led in the wrong direction, rhetoric becomes a lightning rod for the turmoil of feelings in the city experiencing such extreme cultural change. When I say rhetoric is a fundamental element in the cultural revolution of the classical *polis*, this is not just because of its evident role in the law court, say, or the Assembly. The importance of rhetoric is in the way its use and abuse articulate a speaker's view of the world and place in the world – and this is seen at every level of social expression.

In his treatise the *Rhetoric*, Aristotle with his usual formalist zeal divides rhetoric into three branches, *epideictic*, *forensic* and *deliberative*, that is to say, the display pieces associated with the *agora* and theatre (*epideictic*); the legal, competitive arguments associated with the law courts (*forensic*); and the political debating of policy associated with the Assembly (*deliberative*). In each of the following sections of this chapter, I shall be looking at a paradigmatic example of each of these types of speech-making. What I hope will not be forgotten from this first section is that the strategies and language associated with the new intellectuals appear in all the texts of this period, and that while Aristotle's division is a convenient structuring device, rhetoric is a constant informing presence in the city of speech-making.

---

[16] See Stone (1988); Brickhouse and Smith (1989); Euben (1997); Kraut (1984).

II

Gorgias of Leontini in Sicily came to Athens probably for the first time in the early 420s as an ambassador for his city.[17] The story goes that his rhetoric absolutely floored the Athenians with its flair and novelty, and that subsequently he became a celebrated performer and teacher. He was renowned for saying to the audience '*proballe*', 'chuck me a topic' – and then delivering a formal speech off the cuff and with brilliance on whatever the audience suggested. He was said to have died a wealthy man, but anecdotes like this say more about the social prestige of such performers, and the post-Platonic social suspicion of filthy lucre. His influence is widespread: not only is his elaborately balanced and often wildly paradoxical argumentation to be heard echoed in much contemporary writing (and Plato writes a dialogue, *Gorgias*, explicitly against him and rhetoric in general), but also the so-called Second Sophistic, the reflowering of Greek culture in the Roman Empire, took Gorgias as its founding father.

Three works still survive, the *Encomium to Helen*, the *Palamedes*, and *On Not Being*, although this third exists only in reported fragments in different versions in later philosophical compendiums. Sextus Empiricus tells us that *On Not Being* was also known as *On Nature*, and whether this is Gorgias' title or not, it still signals his love of paradox – how could a work on 'nature' be a work on 'what does not exist'? – and the central argument of the piece, as reported, certainly bears out this love of paradox.[18] For he declares first that nothing exists; secondly, if anything exists, it is not apprehensible by man; third, if it is apprehensible, it is inexpressible and uninterpretable by anyone else. It is hard to know what status to afford this tripartite *reductio*. (Sextus Empiricus takes it very seriously indeed; others have been far less sure.) It is certainly radical and polemical. Where Parmenides had argued for the primacy of Being, and Protagoras for 'Man as the measure of all things', and Prodicus for the importance of getting language exactly right, Gorgias dismisses Being – nothing exists – dismisses man's measuring – man cannot apprehend anything – and dismisses the value of language: whatever is apprehended cannot be expressed or interpreted anyway. It is not clear if this leaves Gorgias as a radical relativist, or a radical nihilist – or as an

---

[17] The best introduction to Gorgias is Wardy (1996) which draws also on the studies of Segal (1962); Rosenmeyer (1955).

[18] See Wardy (1996), 6–24 – who has the relevant bibliography also.

extremely sharp parodist of philosophy. Perhaps his parody is so sharp that it raises serious questions about contemporary grand theories about man and language: any doubt about whether you have apprehended Gorgias' seriousness or playfulness seems to *enact* his argument . . .Does Gorgianic seriousness exist, can you apprehend it and can you interpret it?

His speech *Encomium to Helen* offers similar difficulties about how seriously it should be taken: it is certainly a masterpiece of sophistic reversal, irony and paradox.[19] Its aim is to praise Helen of Troy – though a woman in Greece, especially an adulteress, was always open to slander – but its argument spreads its net much wider than the title suggests. It is a paradigm of epideictic rhetoric. Let's look at its opening first:

The *kosmos* of a city is the quality of its men; of a body, its beauty; of a soul, its wisdom; of an action, its excellence; of a speech [*logos*], its truth.[20]

Since Gorgias immediately asserts that 'one should honour with praise what is praiseworthy, but attach blame to the blameworthy', the opening sentence seems to list what might be suitable topics for an encomium: in the case of a city, the fine quality of its men, and so forth. Yet there are two nagging doubts. I did not translate *kosmos*, the first word, because it is hard to capture its range of senses in a single word in English. Its primary meaning is 'order', 'harmony' – so what makes a city a properly ordered city is the good quality of its men. But (as in the English word 'cosmetics'), it can also imply something that is added, false, a mere surface beauty, 'ornament', 'decoration'. Since the speech will turn out to praise Helen, the famously seductive beauty who destroys a city, a woman whose actions and morality are questionable, any ambiguity between proper order and surface attractiveness can hardly be casual. Hence the second doubt: what is the relation between *logos* ('speech', 'argument') and 'truth'? Could 'truth' be called the 'ornament' of speech? Again, in a speech which sets out to praise the apparently unpraisable – and will, as we will see, have much fun with truth – the doubt about how much truth a speech needs will continue to nag.

Gorgias starts his praise with Helen's exceptional parents and wondrous beauty, but passes over the events leading up to the Trojan

---

[19] A text and translation and commentary can be found in MacDowell (1982), though he is well criticized by Wardy (1996), 25–51.
[20] Gorgias, *Encomium* 1.

War with a careful sidestep: 'To tell those who know what they know brings conviction, but does not provide pleasure'.[21] The audience may be flattered by thus being in the know, they may well accept that to be told what they know is indeed easily convincing. But Gorgias has also introduced another criterion here – pleasure. Thucydides rejected the pleasure of easy listening (as we have seen) and tarred Herodotus and others with the accusation of writing for pleasure rather than for truth. Here Gorgias, who set truth as the *kosmos* of a speech, slides towards pleasuring his audience. The negotiation between pleasure and truth will indeed turn out to be the reader's difficulty in this work.

Gorgias moves on to offer four reasons [*aitiai*] why Helen cannot be blamed, four reasons why it is likely/plausible [*eikos*] that she went to Troy. After 'truth' and 'pleasure' we have a third criterion, 'the probable', and once again as in Herodotus and Thucydides, we are scrutinizing causation, or accusation/blame, as *aitia* can also mean. The first reason is that she did what she did by the 'design of fortune and the plot of the gods and the decree of necessity'.[22] The story of the Judgement of Paris and Aphrodite's promise to him is a standard mythic tale. If, as myth has it, Helen was subject to the plotting of the gods and fate itself, how can she be blamed? Gods are greater than human beings, and if humans are subjected to those more powerful, there is no sense in blaming them.

The second reason follows the logic of the mythic tale. If, then, she was seized and raped and humiliated by force, then the perpetrator of the crime is to blame: 'if a woman is raped and deprived of her homeland, how is it reasonable [*eikos*] not to pity her rather than to revile her?'.[23] The logic of the myth is turned against its own regular mistrust and insulting of Helen. If this was – as we still say – the *rape* of Helen, why should she be treated as anything other than a pitiable victim?

The third reason is more complex. If she was persuaded and deceived by *logos*, says the orator, then it is easy to defend her. For:

Logos is a great master which accomplishes the most divine things with the smallest and most invisible body.[24]

The first two reasons had emphasized how force of necessity had compelled Helen to Troy. In Greek, it is standard to oppose persuasion [*peithô*] to force [*bia*] (seduction to rape, diplomacy to military action).[25]

---

[21] Gorgias, *Encomium* 5.   [22] Gorgias, *Encomium* 6.   [23] Gorgias, *Encomium* 7.
[24] Gorgias, *Encomium* 8.   [25] See Buxton (1982).

Gorgias now sets out to collapse that polarity: persuasion is a force which can't be resisted. Persuasion is necessity. Gorgias' bold manipulation of paradox is again dazzling.

How does he maintain such a position? *Logos* has the power, he asserts, to stop fear, to take away grief, to excite joy, and swell pity. Poetry – *logos* with metre, as he defines it – causes the soul to have a unique psychological reaction. So too magic spells have a seductive power. Indeed, many men have been persuaded and have persuaded others into action by forging false arguments. So – and here is the crux of the argument – '*logos* has this self-same power: the *logos* which persuades the soul which it persuades compels it by necessity both to obey what was said and to approve what was done. The one who persuades by using compulsion does wrong, but the woman compelled by speech should not have a bad reputation'.[26] *Logos* is masculine in Greek, soul [*psuchê*] feminine; so it is easy to slide between *logos* and the soul, and Paris and Helen. Each of the verbs applied to *logos*/Paris is active; each applied to Helen/soul is passive. Grammar assists here in making *logos* an irresistible active force. The opposition, so important in Greek thought, between persuasion and compulsion is being effaced. Indeed (§14), what *logos* does to the soul is the same as what a drug does to the body.

In Homer, speech can indeed bewitch and charm; to talk of the power of speech is a commonplace in tragedy;[27] yet here Gorgias makes *logos* a force that cannot be resisted, as if the listeners were passive victims. A great master, indeed. Thucydides' Cleon accused the citizens of the Assembly of behaving like an audience at a sophist show in their passive pleasure – and I have made much of the ideal of the active, critical, participatory role of the citizen of democracy. Here, we see a quite different twist: for the sophist in this performance offers a theorized exposition of an audience's drugged passivity, the victims of *logos* in action.

The fourth reason is just as difficult as the third. If *eros* – sexual desire – was what made her do what she did, no blame can be attached.[28] No blame for a woman who gives in to lust?! This is because – he argues – it is impossible to control what enters the eye and the effect it might have. The soul is *struck*, impressed by what it sees, and as with the fear which affects the viewer of a horrific scene, so Helen experienced a sickness of

---

[26] Gorgias, *Encomium* 12.
[27] See Walsh (1984).
[28] Gorgias, *Encomium* 15.

the soul, a confusion from external sources which rendered her helpless – and thus blameless.

It would be surprising, I think, if the listener to this speech – the spectator at Gorgias' performance – did not worry about the claim that *logos* is irresistible, and that the soul is passive before the force of language and sight. But Gorgias has a final trick up his sleeve. He has, he declares in the final paragraph, achieved what he set out to do in his opening paragraph. He has removed the bad reputation of the woman:

> I have tried to destroy the injustice of the blame and the stupidity of reputation; I wanted to write this speech, an encomium for Helen – but a joke for me![29]

Finally, with the last word Gorgias declares that the speech has been a *paignion*, 'a childish thing', 'a game', 'a joke'. This isn't just a closing wink after a clever performance, but a more far-reaching rhetorical coup – which catches out every reader. Whether you have been persuaded by the argument that *logos* is an irresistible master or not, the twist at the end cocks a snook at your response. For if you *have* been persuaded of a reader's inevitable passivity, now that the joke is out you are revealed as the dupe of the master's *logos*. If, as is more likely, you have *resisted* the argument, as a good critical reader, you are caught missing the joke. If you have just had fun with the speech – then the joke has just worked on you, and *logos* has indeed shown its power over you. It is dizzying trying to work out *how* serious this game with the power of speech is. (It's perhaps no surprise to learn from Aristotle that Gorgias taught that you should undo your opponent's seriousness with laughter, his laughter with seriousness.) Gorgias is a wonderfully manipulative orator who talks about the power of persuasion – and then says you shouldn't take him too seriously. How do you read a seducer who says 'I was only joking'?

Gorgias' epideictic display, then, is not just a boldly witty and paradoxical praise of what might seem impossible to praise. It is also – self-reflexively – *about* the power of *logos*. Yet it does not simply offer a theory about the effects of rhetoric: it sets up and plays with those central ideas of democratic citizenship in the city of words – the critical judgement of the listener and the active/passive role of the citizen in the face of argument. And, most disconcertingly, Gorgias leaves the listener quite at sea with his final shimmy. It is – in all senses – quite a performance.

---

[29] Gorgias, *Encomium* 21.

Gorgias is engaging, frustrating, witty and sophisticated – and also a contemporary of Herodotus and Thucydides, who speak to a shared range of concerns. His manipulative rewriting of myth, his fascination with language in action, his self-conscious dramatization of the politics of culture make him a central figure in the intellectual revolution of Athens.

III

Lysias was an extremely rich metic – a resident alien – who lived and worked in Athens in the last decades of the fifth century and the first decades of the fourth.[30] His father, Cephalus – the host of Plato's *Republic* – was from Syracuse in Sicily, and was persuaded by Pericles (says Lysias himself) to come to Athens. Lysias spent some time in Thurii, the colony whose laws were drawn up by Protagoras and in which Herodotus went to live, before returning to Athens and building up a highly successful shield-manufacturing business. His wealth attracted the attention of the Thirty Tyrants, who murdered his brother and confiscated his property and business. Lysias supported the return of democracy under the leadership of Thrasybulus with financial assistance (and shields), but was never granted citizenship. He was, however, an extremely high-profile speech-writer, and very well connected; and he was sufficiently celebrated as a public figure to be chosen one year to give the public Funeral Oration over the war dead (the same institution for which Thucydides presents Pericles' Funeral Speech). This speech and some thirty others are passed down under his name – several of them incomplete, and several others spurious or of doubtful authorship (including the Funeral Speech). Lysias is the writer whose speech on desire captivates Phaedrus in Plato's *Phaedrus*, and his reputation as the archetypal Attic orator is a commonplace of later literary history – his clarity, propriety, directness, simple diction, and skill in 'smuggling conviction unnoticed past the listener's senses'.[31] For my purposes, I will focus on his writing for the courtroom, which is indeed a perfect example of how forensic oratory is developing under

---

[30] The few facts about Lysias' life are discussed in Carey (1989); Edwards and Usher (1985), which also has texts; and with more technical detail by Dover (1968). For translations see Todd (1996).

[31] Dionysus of Halicarnassus, *Essay on Lysias* 18.

democracy – and I am particularly interested in his strategies for representing character: how is the speaker to present himself?

In Oration 12, *Against Eratosthenes*, Lysias himself is prosecuting the man who arrested and killed his brother on behalf of the tyrants – a speech which immediately shows how difficult it is to maintain any clear division between legal and political oratory.[32] Despite the fact that Lysias is telling his own story here and the violence committed against him and his family, there is very little self-description. In the opening paragraph, he makes the observation – a common one in oratory – that he and his family are not litigious and consequently he worries about his inexperience in public speaking. In the final paragraph, he points out how keenly he has performed his civic duties, restoring the temples which the tyrants despoiled, supporting the city they humiliated, and restoring the dockyards which they had destroyed. At the opening and close of the speech, that is, he appears dressed in the standard clothing of the good citizen who has performed his obligations fully (for all that he is technically a 'metic', a resident alien). It is, however, the main body of the speech which is more revealing of Lysias' strategies of representation.

The first strategy is to construct a narrative which encourages the jury to see events from Lysias' point of view. This is achieved primarily by a vivid, clear, engaging first-person narrative of the fateful days of the tyranny. Lysias has been seized and put under guard in the house of one Damnippos:

Such was my position that I decided to take a chance, as it looked like death for me. I called over Damnippos and said 'You are my friend; I've come into your home; I've done no wrong; I'm in a terrible situation; so please use your power to save me!'[33]

Lysias uses the lure of the adventure story – with himself as its central character, its hero – to create a particular picture for his audience, seen through Lysias' eyes. Damnippos goes off to talk to the other guard, and

while he was talking (I happened to be familiar with the house and knew it had a back door), I decided to try for safety . . .there were three doors for me to pass through, and all happened to be open. When I got to the house of the sea-captain, I sent to town to find out about my brother. He came back and said that Eratosthenes had arrested him in the street and taken him off to prison.[34]

There is scarcely an adjective or an adverb here, and scarcely even a

---

[32] See Ober (1989); Cartlege, Millett, Todd edd. (1990); Cohen (1991).
[33] Lysias 12. 14.
[34] Lysias 12. 16.

moral judgement, even as Lysias articulates the risks of fleeing and represents his desperate negotiations with his friend and guard. At one level, this account is designed to create a 'reality effect' – an authoritative presentation of facts, the facts that will convict Eratosthenes. At another level, attracting the jury into Lysias' point of view is part of his strategy of objectifying Eratosthenes – making him into an object (of disgust, scorn, outrage) for the jury, and thus preventing them seeing his point of view. This strategy is seen in a battery of second-person addresses ('If you were a good man, Eratosthenes . . .')[35] and third-person assaults ('He seems to me to be capable of any sort of rashness, when he comes before judges who have suffered at his hands . . .').[36] Indeed, he even brilliantly turns Eratosthenes' own self-defence against him. Eratosthenes claims that he had spoken against the murder in the Council and had been forced by fear to act. Lysias appears to accept this justification – only sharply to turn it back into a bitterly precise insistence on the fact of murder:

I do not wish to avoid your claim. I agree with you, if you like, that you opposed the murder. But I wonder what you would have done if you had supported the motion, since when you opposed it, you killed Polemarchus![37]

Lysias contrasts the simple, bare, swift account of his own activity with the full array of moral outrage, aggressive accusation and politically charged vehemence when it comes to setting Eratosthenes as a character before the judgement of the jury. In this way, Lysias constructs himself as the exemplary victim of tyranny, a democratic figure who has suffered with the people who make up the jury and whose unalloyed suffering proves the full horror of the tyrant's behaviour. Lysias' political self-representation is carefully calibrated to target the jury on the need to punish Eratosthenes for the city's good. Hence his extraordinary concluding sentence:

I will stop my prosecution. You have heard; you have seen; you have suffered; you hold the men. Judge them![38]

The list 'you have heard; you have seen; you have suffered' links the prosecution's speech to the violent experiences of the jury: the jury's suffering is made to stand as the validation of Lysias' speech. The perfect-tense verbs shift suddenly into the present with *ekhete*, 'you hold

---

[35] Lysias 12. 32.
[36] Lysias 12. 84.
[37] Lysias 12. 34.
[38] Lysias 12. 100: *akêkoate, heorâkate, peponthate, ekhete, dikazete.*

[the men]' – a blunt declaration – and then, with imposing finality, the imperative 'Judge [them]!', *dikazete*. The sequence of verbs seems to demand an inevitable transition from hearing the case to judging the accused guilty. And that, of course, is Lysias' aim.

The speech against Eratosthenes is the only courtroom speech we have in which Lysias speaks in his own voice, on his own behalf. In Athenian courts (unlike Roman legal proceedings) each prosecutor and each defendant had to speak for himself; there were no professional advocates.[39] But this did not stop a citizen from hiring a *logographos*, a speech-writer, to prepare his case. Lysias' other forensic speeches are of this sort. Oration 1 was written on behalf of a man called Euphiletus who had caught a man called Eratosthenes (not the same fellow as the tyrant!) in bed with his wife, and killed him. We have seen Gorgias' defence of the adulteress, Helen. Here we have the cuckold's defence of revenge. The prosecution claims that he had entrapped Eratosthenes with premeditation. Euphiletus defends himself on the grounds that the law specifies that if a husband catches an adulterer in the act and kills him, he should not be prosecuted for murder – a law he supports with a further statute which itemizes a more serious punishment for seduction than for rape. The details of the legal issues are complex and I will not discuss them here.[40] My interest again is with Lysias' strategies of representation for the speaker, Euphiletus.

The speech is clearly and simply constructed in formal terms, in a way which became standard for the later rhetorical schools. It has a brief prologue which sets up the case and the speaker's relationship with the jury; a central narrative; followed by a legal/moral judgement and proof of fact based on the narrative; followed by a brief conclusion, with a plea for justice. Where Oration 12, a prosecution speech, set out the perpetrator for display before the gaze of the jury, this speech of defence needs different strategies of presentation. What's more, as a husband whose wife was seduced by another man, and a man who has to prove that he had no foreknowledge of his wife's sexual deception, Euphiletus' self-representation before a jury of Athenian men is not necessarily a straightforward business.

Lysias begins by lining the speaker up with the jury: 'I would most appreciate it, gentlemen, if, as the jurors in this case, you would adopt the same attitude to me as you would to yourselves if you had faced a

---

[39] For all the facts on Athenian legal process see Todd (1993).
[40] See Omitowoju (2002) with extensive bibliography, and Cohen (1991), 98–170.

similar experience'.[41] In making such an appeal for sympathy, what is taken for granted is that anyone could have been in Euphiletus' position: the circumstances are not unique or remarkable but readily understandable. Euphiletus is going to stress repeatedly that he acted not only within the law, not only for the benefit of the state, but also just as any normal man would be expected to act. His narrative indeed emphasizes the normality – *to eikos* – of his situation. When he married, he says, he was neither too domineering nor too liberal, but 'looked over her as much as is reasonable [*eikos*]'.[42] In those early days, he thought her the best of wives, 'a wonderful housekeeper, thrifty, and managing everything to a nicety'.[43] What any man would want in a wife . . . The audience's expectations are being run in line with the speaker's case. This rather simple self-characterization continues, as he fills in the necessary details for his story: 'first, gentlemen, – I had better tell you these facts – I have a little two-storey house, upstairs and downstairs the same, women's quarters upstairs, men's downstairs.'[44] The apology for relaying such mundane facts, the simple dwelling, the rather limping description of the living arrangements carefully portray an ordinary man in very ordinary surroundings. So, when the baby was born, the mother nursed it – no wet nurse, as in upper-class households – and so that she could feed it without disturbing her husband, the women moved downstairs – and so they lived: 'I was so naive' he concludes 'that I thought my wife the most respectable [*sôphronestatê*] woman in the city'.[45] His confession of naivety, the innocence of a man who just trusts his wife – remember that Odysseus is praised in the *Odyssey* for testing even Penelope – also hints to the audience that self-satisfaction ought not to be a husband's lot. As Semonides wrote back in the archaic period in his satire on women: 'The woman who seems particularly to be respectable [*sôphrôn*] is the one who also does the most harm'.[46] For everyone thinks it is only his neighbour's wife who is awful. The dim reflection of this popular wisdom – no poetic quotation, of course – also adds to the persuasive characterization of Euphiletus, and the recognizable moral framing of his story.

This naivety continues through the narrative, with a lovely picture of their domestic banter. One night, when the baby was screaming downstairs – he learnt later that it was being teased to make it cry to help his

[41] Lysias 1. 1.   [42] Lysias 1. 6.   [43] Lysias 1. 7.
[44] Lysias 1. 9.   [45] Lysias 1. 10.
[46] Semonides 7. 108–9, brilliantly discussed by Loraux (1993), 72–110.

wife's plotting – Euphiletus told her to go down and feed the child to stop the crying:

At first she didn't want to, as if she was so pleased to see me back after my time away. When I got angry and told her to go down, she said 'So that you can have a go at the maid! You grabbed her once before when you were drunk!' I laughed, and she got up, shut the door as she left, pretending to lark about, and turned the key. I thought nothing of this, I had no suspicions, and slept happily . . .[47]

This pointedly homely tale is complex in the message it gives to the jury. It certainly portrays the husband's naivety: he lets himself be locked into his own bedroom while his wife goes down to her lover – and he repeats the story for us. Could this man have been involved in a premeditated plot of murder? At the same time, it presents him as an ordinary fellow – asking, then ordering his wife to go downstairs to see to the baby; pleased that she is pleased to see him. What's more, when he was drunk, he manhandled the maid. This is neither the scandalous debauchery of an Alcibiades nor the paraded chastity of a philosopher. The very form of the anecdote, with the easy vividness of the direct quotation from his wife, and with the casually mundane details, produces a carefully persuasive image of 'everyday life': something shared with the jury. He's the sort of man who might get drunk and fool around – but not a premeditated murderer. The enthymeme, for Aristotle, is an argument based on an audience's sense of *to eikos*: this whole narrative acts as a projection of *to eikos* to ground Euphiletus' self-representation as believeable, as authoritative.

The narrative unfurls with Euphiletus being tipped off, coming home with friends, finding Eratosthenes with his wife, and taking revenge:

I tied his hands behind him and asked him why he was in my house and committing this outrage. He confessed his crime, and begged and supplicated me not to kill him but to take money in settlement. I replied 'It is not I who will kill you, but the law of the city, which you are transgressing. You rate it less than your pleasures, and chose to commit such a terrible crime against my wife and against my children rather than obey the laws and be in order [*kosmios*]'. Thus, gentlemen, that man met with what the law orders for such criminals.[48]

The climactic moment of revenge is carefully stage-managed both to elicit a confession, and, perhaps most importantly, to emphasize that Euphiletus acts as the agent of law. The direct speech now rings with the authority of a herald's announcement, as Euphiletus delivers summary

[47] Lysias 1. 12.
[48] Lysias 1. 25–6.

judgement for the witnesses and now the jury. Where a modern narrative would always be tempted to portray a scene of adultery and revenge as a moment of personal trauma and emotional crisis, Lysias has Euphiletus describe the outrage as 'entering the house' and a crime committed against his wife and children – an attack, that is, on the sanctity of marriage itself, the cornerstone of the household.[49] Indeed, the threat of seduction, as opposed to rape, explains Euphiletus, is precisely that it brings 'the whole house' under the sway of the adulterer. 'Pleasure' is opposed to 'law', 'transgression' to 'propriety' – but what is at stake here is not the ins-and-outs of the emotional life of loving adults, but the social order of the city. As Euphiletus opens his conclusion, 'this punishment is not a personal issue for my benefit, but enacted on behalf of the whole city'.[50] The need to deny personal involvement indicates an expectation of its relevance; yet the recognition that the social and sexual behaviour of every citizen contributes to the order [*kosmos*] of the city, and is scrutinized and regulated as such, is a commonplace in classical Athens not just of the courtroom. Especially as it enters court, the ordinary man's homelife becomes a political issue. Euphiletus cannot represent himself just as an ordinary man; he must also be seen to be a good citizen. Euphiletus lines up with the jury as citizens doing their civic duty in the shared project of maintaining the justice of the state.

The courts of Athens were not only institutions for the resolution of conflict, nor for the defining of law through precedent and test cases. While major murder trials, like the defence of Euphiletus or the prosecution of Eratosthenes, may seem at first sight recognizably similar to modern courtroom proceedings, as do the many ancient financial and inheritance cases, it would be misleading to think of the Athenian legal system as being the same as the modern western courtroom. It's not just that the courts are all-male affairs with large juries, chosen by lot, with no judges or professional lawyers. What is perhaps most distinctive about the ancient Athenian courts is that they formed an arena where elite males competed with each other in status and position.[51] So Demosthenes and Aeschines clash in a series of huge trials over a period of fifteen years. Some of the charges may seem trivial: Aeschines makes a prosecution for the technical offence that Demosthenes was presented with a crown at the Great Dionysia, an illegal setting for such a presentation. This trial, however, prompted Demosthenes to write

---

[49] Tanner (1980) is unsurpassed here.
[50] Lysias 1. 47.
[51] See Todd (1993); Cartledge, Millett, Todd edd. 1990); Cohen (1991); Ober (1989).

what turned out to be his longest and possibly his most famous and influential speech, *On the Crown*. When Aeschines lost this case, he was forced into exile. Some of the most heated debates about Athenian policy with regard to the rising power of Macedon, ruled by Philip, took place in trials over the correct behaviour of members of the embassies to Philip's court. These are major political battles between the leading politicians of democracy. But even what seem to be more private cases turn out to involve such conflicts between men. *On Neaira* is technically a prosecution of a woman, Neaira, accusing her of not being a citizen's daughter, but a prostitute.[52] It is a case which viciously assaults Neaira, for sure, but which is also the attempt of one Apollodorus to attack his personal enemy Stephanos, who was married to the unfortunate Neaira.

It is partly this intense political competitiveness which makes rhetoric – speaking well in court – so important an element in democracy's institutional proceedings. There is a lot at stake for a citizen in court. The authority that comes from success in public forums stems from an ability to present oneself convincingly in and through rhetorical performance. Lysias is a master of such representation – the construction of authority through character and narrative. Within the suspicious, conflict-laden, challenging sphere of courtroom debate, he is an expert in finding the narrative which engages and draws the jury into his construction of *to eikos*, and superb at framing his arguments so that the figure of the speaker emerges not just as a good citizen but as the hero – the authoritative hero – of his own plausible narrative.

What rhetoric also brings is an acute self-consciousness about the power of language. To speak in court is to engage in a competitive environment where the jury is fully aware of a speaker's attempts to persuade, and the speakers are aware of the jury's resistance to being convinced, as well as the competition between himself and other speakers. The courtroom becomes a self-reflexive, self-aware battleground for control over the narrative of *to eikos* – who can claim the most plausible story, who can stake for himself a convincing position, who can best manipulate the insinuation that his opponent is untrustworthy and deceptive. Rhetoric, especially in the hands of a Lysias, is not a question of deploying some standard techniques, some lines from the textbook. When the speaker and the listener know the standard techniques, how persuasive are such moves likely to be? Rhetoric is – as Gorgias knows –

---

[52] Transmitted to us as Demosthenes 59, but written by Apollodorus. For text, translation and commentary see Carey (1992).

a more seductive business, where, as Dionysius of Halicarnassus says of Lysias, the skill is in 'smuggling conviction unnoticed past the listener's senses'. Sly manipulation – veiled power – is the necessary companion to the self-consciousness of rhetoric. With the knowledge of rhetoric comes an inevitable knowingness of performance.

Gorgias plays – however seriously – with language's power and his audience's engaged response; Thucydides displays for the reader's evaluation the misprisions and violent consequences of political rhetoric in the state; Lysias' courtroom speeches, however, are testimony of the life-and-death struggles of citizens fought out with words before a judging public. This is the new technique of prose in action at the very heart of democracy's institutional machine.

IV

Demosthenes is undoubtedly the most distinguished orator of the classical city. He was born in 384 – a full generation after Gorgias, Thucydides and Lysias – and his active political life was thus not only in the developed democracy of the fourth century, but also in the era of Macedon's growth to dominance in Greece under Philip and then Alexander the Great.[53] He spoke repeatedly against Philip in a series of foreign-policy orations (especially in the series known as the *Philippics*, imitated by Cicero against Mark Antony, from which we get the word 'philippic' for any political broadside). His orations were regarded as the models for later orators, and because of his fame, there is a series of anecdotes about him, which are also central to the image of the orator. Plutarch's *Life of Demosthenes*, for example, rehearses the stories that he trained himself for the disruptions of the Assembly by speaking on the beach at the sea (others add 'with stones in his mouth'); he retired to a cave to study and shaved half his head to keep himself there; to correct an awkward shoulder gesture when speaking, he practised with a dagger hanging from the ceiling to stop his shoulder moving; he had a full-length mirror, in front of which he rehearsed each speech. It is striking that all these tales – and there are more besides – are about the orator's training and practice of self-presentation. For all the openness of democracy's invitation 'Who wishes to speak?', spontaneity

---

[53] For the biography and its bibliography see e.g. Sealey (1993), and as a more general background Strauss (1987).

is rigorously subordinated to preparation, not just in argument but also in self-image. So, when asked for the most important element in good oratory, Demosthenes replied '*hupokrisis*'; when asked for the second most important element, he replied '*hupokrisis*'; when asked for the third, he replied '*hupokrisis*'. *Hupokrisis* means 'self-presentation in performance'. (It is sometimes rather weakly translated as 'delivery' – but it is a term linked to the world of the actor on stage [*hupokritês*] and indicates what the orator has borrowed from the theatre.)[54] The anecdotal tradition about Demosthenes echoes the rhetorical handbooks in insisting that the self-representation of an orator is central to the success of any argument.

Demosthenes was a leading *rhêtôr* – a word usually translated either 'orator' or 'politician'. The *rhêtôr* was a man in the public eye who became influential on public policy by his speaking in the Assembly and the Courts and the Council – hence the double translation 'orator/ politician'.[55] There were no formal political parties in Athens – though there were shifting alliances of different *rhêtores* and their supporters, and foreign policy, say, could create groups of citizens who, for example, supported war or appeasement. Demosthenes clashed in particular with Aeschines, another leading *rhêtôr* (who had been an actor – which also helps focus attention on *hupokrisis*). They clashed over the issue of how to respond to Macedonia's imperialism, and, as I have already mentioned, the two fought out this political disagreement over at least fifteen years.

This battle was not just a matter of policy, but of personal status and power, and was conducted through the courts with a committed vehemence. Aeschines successfully prosecuted (in 345) one of Demosthenes' supporters, Timarchus, on the grounds that he had been a male prostitute as a youth and thus should be debarred from citizenship. It's a speech full of wonderfully sly innuendo, mixed with a good degree of vitriole, and it was wholly successful.[56] Timarchus had been about to prosecute Aeschines (with Demosthenes' assistance) for corruption on an embassy to Philip – and so Aeschines' pre-emptive strike was also an act of self-defence: as a non-citizen Timarchus could no longer bring his prosecution of Aeschines to court. In 343, however,

---

[54] See Hall (1995).
[55] See Connor (1971) for a good introduction to this.
[56] Discussed at length in Winkler (1990), 45–70, Dover (1978), and Davidson (1997) (whose criticisms of Foucault in particular are tendentious), with background discussion in Halperin (1990), 88–112 and Cohen (1991), 171–202. See now Fisher (2001).

Demosthenes himself brought a case against Aeschines on the same charge that he had committed treason by accepting pay from Philip during this embassy and beyond. Demosthenes lost the case, and Aeschines' speech of defence includes some hilarious portrayals of Demosthenes on the diplomatic mission, including the time when the famous orator dried in front of Philip – who gently encouraged him to keep his cool. But finally, when Aeschines in 330 prosecuted Ctesiphon, the man who had proposed the award of a crown to Demosthenes, Demosthenes' slashingly brilliant *On the Crown* forced Aeschines into exile. The defeat of Athens at the battle of Chaeronea and Macedon's dominance is a fundamental context for this shift of public opinion away from the man who had supported Philip and towards the figure who had fought and lost against such dominance. These speeches show how orations for the court can be political in the strongest sense of the public debate of major state policy and the construction of the authority of the leading actors in state policy. All the various strategies which are used to project and promote the authority of the political orator are vividly displayed and manipulated.

One of the defining tensions in Athenian political life is between the ideal of equality enshrined in democratic principle and the competitive pursuit of personal glory basic to Greek culture. The politicians almost invariably come from the elite echelons of society, but are competing before the mass of citizens. From what position can the elite speaker persuade the mass audience that he speaks authoritatively not just to them but for them? How can the privileged *rhêtôr* present himself as *dêmotikos*, 'of and for the people'?[57] The very distinction between prose and poetry is utilized in a fascinating way amid the multiform twists and turns of democratic rhetorical imaging. Aeschines, for example, dramatically predicts the performance of one of Timarchus' witnesses:

In the defence's case, one of the generals will mount the platform, I hear, head held high with a self-regarding expression, like a man born to the wrestling school and philosophy class . . . He will try and ridicule the trial . . . as the beginning of a terrible lack of culture. He will not even leave out the poems of Homer, they say, and the names of the heroes, but will celebrate the friendship of Achilles and Patroclus, said to have a sexual basis.[58]

Aeschines offers a sneering portrait of one of the leading military and political figures of the state speaking in defence of Timarchus against the

---

[57] Fine discussion in Ober (1989).
[58] Aeschines 1. 132–3. On the use of Homer in court see Ford (1999).

charge of homosexual prostitution by recalling the grand literary model of the heroes Achilles and Patroclus, whose friendship was, by the fifth century at least, seen as an erotic liaison. The snobbery of the general is instantly established by his self-presentation of 'head held high' and 'self-regarding expression'. He has an upper-class education (scoffs Aeschines) in the exclusive world of the gym and philosophy circle. For such a person, this trial is not about the essence of citizenship but an issue of being 'cultivated'. In contrast, Aeschines claims that any man who could sell his own body is so corrupt and so alien to the democratic principles of autonomy and self-control that he could sell the state too. He depicts the general, however, as citing Homer as an authority for Timarchus' scandalous erotic behaviour. Aeschines will go on to offer his own understanding of Homer, but, ironically enough, this does not stop him from slurring the general for not being one of the people – and taking his use of poetry as a sign of upper-class exclusivity. Here we see the orator with a democratic sneer turning the tension between mass and elite to his own favour.

Demosthenes can turn this rhetoric of poetry back against Aeschines, however. In the speech *On The Corrupt Embassy*, he quotes Creon's speech from Sophocles' *Antigone* – a speech about the testing of a political leader in a crisis – to scoff that Aeschines, a former actor, appears to have learnt nothing from playing such a role.[59] Similarly in *On The Crown* he quotes an epigram inscribed on stone by the state to mark the death of its citizens in battle, dead over whom Demosthenes had been chosen to give the Funeral Oration. Quoting this state-sponsored poem is to show Aeschines' 'lack of judgement, hypocrisy and disgustingness'.[60] The poetry of tragedy – the people's festival – and the poetry of public inscription can be cited to humiliate Aeschines, the former actor, whose very vocal skills indicate his untrustworthy hypocrisy. Aeschines can even be denigrated by Demosthenes because being an actor makes him less of a citizen:

you used to teach writing, when I went to school; you performed initiations, I was initiated; you were a clerk, I spoke in the Assembly; you were the third actor, I was in the audience.[61]

Each of these paired phrases is designed to revile Aeschines and parade Demosthenes' good citizenship. So where Aeschines was a

---

[59] Dem. 19. 247–50.
[60] Dem. 18. 289.
[61] Dem. 18. 265.

humble teacher, an assistant in religious rites, a clerk to the Assembly, an actor on stage – all, it is suggested, lowly jobs in the democratic institutional world – Demosthenes studied, spoke at public meetings, took part in religious rituals and was in the audience of the tragedy festival. The ideals of participatory citizenship are aggressively displayed. To be 'one of the people' does not necessarily mean presenting oneself as a humble or lowly man. The whole audience can aspire to the ideals of fully playing the proper role of citizen and can join in the mocking of the inadequate. The citizen in the jury or Assembly can idealize his own values, attitudes and behaviour. The politics of culture can be manipulated in the public arena with differing rhetorics of exclusion and inclusion. Hence the twists and turns of the violent and bitter exchanges in public about what it is to fulfil the role of citizen.

This patterning of exclusion and inclusion also structures the speeches Demosthenes makes before the Assembly. These are speeches proposing a particular course of action to the Athenians, and they have little of the competitive vitriole of the courtroom. They do produce a consistent and powerful picture of Philip as a looming and insidiously clever force, but the fundamental purpose is to win over the mass of citizens to Demosthenes' view of what must be done. Here is a paragraph from the celebrated opening of the first *Olynthiac*, a speech trying to encourage the Athenians to offer military aid to Olynthus, a town threatened by Philip's imperialism:

The present crisis, men of Athens, all but shouts that you yourselves must take control of these affairs if you care about their security. But we seem to have an attitude towards them I can't fathom. These are my opinions: to vote help [for Olynthus] now; and to make the speediest preparation for you to send it from here; you must not suffer what happened before. An embassy should also be sent to announce this and to oversee matters. The danger is that this man, unscrupulous and clever as he is at turning matters to his own advantage, conceding here, threatening there (it's likely he'll seem convincing!), and slandering us and our absence, may work to seize some major advantage for himself. Yet in all likelihood, men of Athens, what's hardest to fight against in Philip's dealings, is also best for you . . .[62]

The main proposal of the speech is set firmly at its head: an expedition and a diplomatic mission; action now. So too is the portrayal of Philip as a dangerous and manipulative enemy. What is also striking, however, is the way Demosthenes *works* his audience. He begins by addressing them forcefully in the second person: 'you yourselves' must

[62] Dem. 1.2.

act if 'you care' about the issue. But this immediately moves to an inclusive first person plural: '*we* seem to have an attitude' – an inclusivity from which he disengages himself, 'which I can't fathom'. This prepares for *his* opinion – offered thus as if this is a shared discussion (rather than a prepared policy statement). It is the audience, however, who must act: 'you' are to send help, and thus 'not suffer what you did before' (when the advice of Demosthenes was not followed!). The description of Philip's diplomacy ('conceding here, threatening there') becomes an exercise in complicity as Demosthenes glosses the threat for his audience with a 'you all know' glance – *eikotôs*: 'it's what we all expect, isn't it?' Philip's slanders are directed at this complicit group: 'he attacks *us* and *our* absence'. Yet, Demosthenes continues, I can show *you* how what seems worst about Philip may be best for *you*. From a shared position ('in all likelihood', that is, what we agree upon [*epieikôs*]), Demosthenes offers a paradoxical riddle – how can what is worst be best? – which he himself will solve, thus establishing himself as an authority for the audience: the man with the answer. Demosthenes strives to produce a collective with himself at the head.

This detailed analysis – which the paragraph needs – reveals how carefully manipulative Demosthenes' rhetoric of address is. He pulls his audience in, pushes them away, cajoles, prods, makes them complicit. Self-presentation here is constructing a relation between the 'I' of the speaker, the 'you' of the audience, and the 'we' which makes the decision Demosthenes wants.

The final paragraph of the speech is the climax of this process:

Every person who considers every one of these issues must help and push away war from here. The rich, so that by expending a small amount for the sake of the plenty they possess in their good fortune may enjoy its fruits in future without fear; those in their prime, so that by obtaining an experience of war in Philip's territory they may become fearsome guards of an untouched homeland; the orators, so that the inspection of their political lives may be easy, as whatever affairs surround you, you will be such critics of what has been done by them. May these things be good for the sake of all.[63]

At the close, the collective is all. *Everyone* looking at *every* issue is enlisted to Demosthenes' proposal. 'Everyone' is broken down into categories. The rich will benefit by keeping their plenty without danger in the future; the men who make up the army will fight not on Attic soil, and thus learn to value all the more the good of the homeland; the

---

[63] Dem. 1. 28.

orators/politicians will have an easy ride fom the people. These interest groups in the third person – and note that no-one is described as 'poor' or 'incapable' – give way to 'you' – the second-person address – who are brought into the frame as 'judges' [*kritai*] of events. The responsibility of voting is thus underlined as the duty of the evaluating citizen – as the turn from the third person to the second person seems to allow each citizen to exclude himself from the interest groups of the rich, the soldiers, the politicians. Now what is at stake is the *common*wealth. Demosthenes' rhetoric works to place everyone in the same collective, working for the same common good – by following Demosthenes' agenda. That the Athenians huffed and puffed but failed to follow Demosthenes' advice of swift and decisive action is a reminder of the uncertainty of rhetoric's success. It is the precariousness of rhetoric's power to persuade that gives these political exchanges their thrill and danger, for speakers and audiences alike.

Demosthenes is much less commonly read in schools and universities these days than in previous centuries, when rhetoric constituted a basis of formal education, and Demosthenes' oratory was a standard model for public life (one of the essentials of a classical education). This silencing is a pity, not least because Demosthenes (and Aeschines and the other orators) offer the social and cultural historian such a telling insight into the public media in and through which democracy functioned. Demosthenes' self-presentation – and the presentation of his opponents – reveals the struggle to claim the personal authority of a good citizen, the authority to speak and to be heard as a good citizen. This is a struggle which is enacted constantly within the self-conscious awareness of rhetoric's power to deceive and to persuade: the complex relation between politicians, their opponents, and the audience of judging citizens makes rhetoric an intricate, risky game of manipulation and resistance, a game of immense seriousness and political importance. Yet rhetoric – spin, propaganda, advertising, performance – is not alien nor a threat to democracy.[64] The institutions of democracy depend on the public exchange of competing views. The belief that such views can just be expressed clearly and cleanly, man to man, without the veils of persuasiveness, for a disinterested decision, is at best a rhetorical claim, at worst a naive and dangerous fantasy. Demosthenes' prose shows with extraordinary vividness the necessarily veiled and manipulative interconnections of power and performance in democracy. It is through the

---

[64] Very well discussed by Hesk (2000).

writing and performance of this prose that the politics of democracy was enacted.

V

For the final section of this chapter, I want to turn to the formalization of rhetoric as a 'science' or discipline [*technê*]. As soon as rhetoric is recognized as a subject, it is associated with a problem of how it is to be taught. In Homer, the standard ideal of heroism is expressed as 'to be a speaker of speeches and a doer of deeds', and not only is Odysseus celebrated as the master of words for his tricky persuasiveness, but also Nestor and other elders are singled out for their abilities in counsel as wise speakers.[65] Yet it is only with the invention of rhetoric as a discipline that 'teaching' becomes a specific problem. Greeks loved to tell stories about the 'first inventor' of things. Rhetoric's inventors were said to be Corax and Tisias, in Sicily; and the first story of rhetoric is precisely an anecdote of teaching as a scene of paradigmatic difficulty. Corax was Tisias' teacher; Tisias refused to pay his bill. Corax took him to court. Tisias argued that if he could not persuade the jury of the correctness of his case, then clearly Corax had taught him nothing and thus there was no need to pay; but if Corax had taught him well, then he would be able to convince the jury – that he owed Corax nothing. Rhetoric's founding tale, then, is of the rhetoric teacher hoist on his own paradox.

The dodgy teacher of rhetoric is a commonplace of comedy; a fear of conservative polemics; and a source of innumerable anecdotes. Yet rhetoric rapidly becomes a central plank of Greek and then Roman education throughout the West – part of the cultural glue of the educated/civilized. I want to look briefly here at two contrasting figures who are known as great teachers of rhetoric in very different ways. The first is Isocrates, who was roughly contemporary with Plato; the second is Aristotle, student of Plato, who founded the Lyceum, a school to rival Plato's Academy. I have introduced these two in relation to Plato because both are integrally connected with him and with his attacks on rhetoric in the name of philosophy. For Isocrates calls himself a philosopher, for all that he offers great exemplars of rhetoric. Aristotle, with precise control, repeatedly criticizes his great master from a

---

[65] See Cole (1991), 33–46; and especially Martin (1989).

theoretical and practical perspective. Where Plato wanted to ban rhetoric and theatre from his ideal Republic, Aristotle writes his *Poetics* which justifies the educational role of tragedy. Together, Isocrates and Aristotle show how rhetoric becomes a discipline rather than just a name for persuasive speaking.

The corpus of Isocrates consists in a quite different type of material from the orators we have seen so far in this chapter. It is difficult to know if any of his orations were actually performed by Isocrates (or anyone else).[66] Several have performance contexts, in that they are written as if they are speeches for particular occasions. The most famous of those is the *Panegyricus* which is written as if for the hundreth Olympic games (380 BCE). While speeches were delivered at this great public arena (and both Gorgias and Lysias are said to have addressed the assembled Greek peoples there), Isocrates' speech runs to some fifty pages, in very carefully polished prose, and was said to have taken ten years to complete. Whether Isocrates ever spoke at Olympia or not, this work was designed to be circulated as a written text. It is a political pamphlet in the form of an oration. It calls for the Greek cities to give up fighting each other in what he regards as suicidal wars of petty rivalry, and appeals for a spirit of Panhellenism to breathe through Greek politics. Greeks should unite against the barbarians. But this project needs leadership, and Isocrates mounts a campaign for Athens to regain its hegemony because of its unique history in resisting the Persians and because of its unique contributions to culture.

It will be obvious that we are in very similar territory to that covered by Herodotus with his view of the clash of Greeks and barbarians; and by Thucydides, with his view of the importance of the image of Athens as epitomized in Pericles' Funeral Speech; and by Demosthenes, with his assertive foreign policy. Isocrates moulds an image of the past – Athens already has a 'classical' history – together with an idealism about Greek cultural achievement – where philosophy reigns supreme – together with a generalized political agenda of collective action against the barbarian other – without, that is, any of the pressing and precise political judgements of a Demosthenes. This mixture proved extremely fruitful: this speech is much read, imitated and highly influential in the history of political rhetoric. It is in this way – rather than by affecting policy directly – that Isocrates is a teacher. His exemplary speeches are to help produce orators.

[66] Discussed by Too (1995).

Tellingly, Isocrates states directly that rhetoric cannot be a matter of a fixed set of rules easily communicated to a pupil (something that many later writers have not understood), but is rather an ability to discover a novel case that fits the present circumstances. Rhetoric by definition is an act of performance *in context*. Education – training – makes men more technically proficient [*tekhnikôteroi*] and more ready [*euporôteroi*], but it cannot fashion men who lack natural aptitude into good debaters or good composers of speeches.[67] What is needed thus is 'natural ability' combined with solid 'training in practical expertise' [*tois peri tês empeiriâs gegumnasmenois*] – spending time, that is, with a teacher like Isocrates. *Gegumnasmenos* – literally 'exercised' as in the gym – gives precisely the model Isocrates wants. Rhetoric, like the gym, requires training for success and talent, but you cannot hope to draw up a simple list of do's and don'ts to make a successful sporting hero.

This process of training is wonderfully encapsulated in another of Isocrates' huge display pieces, the *Panathenaicus* – almost eighty pages long – written as if for the festival of the Panathenaea of 342 BCE (started when Isocrates was 93 years old!).[68] Towards the end of this speech, he announces that he had written what we have just been reading and was revising it, when he decided to show it to some of his pupils. He then dramatizes a long and complex exchange. His students praise the speech wondrously, but one was clearly unhappy. Isocrates asks why – and the pupil indicates that what has been written about Sparta seems to him to be insulting to that great nation. Isocrates lets rip and aggressively corrects his student. The student accepts the rebuff with sophisticated tact – but Isocrates continues to worry about the critique. Indeed, after some further discussion with his clique of pupils he confesses: 'I had perhaps debated effectively, but for that very reason I had shown less intelligence and more pride than befits a man of my age'.[69] So he dictates a further ending to the speech and summons the class again to hear what has been composed. This time the precocious student offers an extended reading of the whole speech, in order to show that Isocrates had in fact a concealed meaning running through the speech, which only the careful and sophisticated reader would pick up. There was covert praise for Sparta – since, in the current political climate, praise for Sparta must be covert. The rest of the class lavishly

---

[67] *Against the Sophists* 15.
[68] For bibliography and more extensive discussion of the material of the next paragraphs, see Goldhill (1999).
[69] Isocrates 5. 230.

praise the student's penetrating interpretation – but Isocrates, he himself tells us, praised the boy's abilities as a speaker, but said nothing about his grand idea, neither whether this 'covert meaning' was right, nor whether it was wrong. Thus the reader is left to make his or her own judgement about the exchange: has the pupil correctly divined the master's strategy by virtue of his careful and sophisticated reading, or is the pupil a model of misplaced ingenuity and error?

The point of this long exercise in dramatized interpretation and counter-interpretation is brought home in the final paragraph. Isocrates explains that this speech is written for those who consider that orations which are written for educational and exemplary disciplinary purposes [*didaskalos kai tekhnikos*] have more serious and philosophical weight than pieces written for display [*epideiktikos*] or for the law court.[70] But, and this is most important, any reader must not merely trust his or her own judgement and accept the views of lazy readers. Reading and interpretation require critical expertise and study.

Here we find a full-scale picture of Isocrates' rhetoric in action. It is, first of all, *didaskalos* and *tekhnikos*, an educational tool, designed to give technical expertise through training in a discipline. This is in explicit contrast to epideictic and forensic oratory. Isocrates' rhetorical practice is designed to produce not just good speakers but readers who are not lazy but sophisticated, not hasty but critical. Isocrates aims to produce the good citizen of democracy – that critical, evaluative audience and performer – through a training in the production and reception of *logos*.

That Isocrates is concerned with a general moral message and not just with rhetorical skill is clear throughout his work. Apart from the great political orations I have mentioned, and his speeches for the law court, including a long self-defence which recalls Plato's *Apology*, he also writes letters to major political figures, such as Philip of Macedon, Alexander the Great, and Nicocles, the son and heir of Evagoras of Cyprus (a great ruler in Isocrates' judgement). These are open addresses that discuss what makes a good ruler. This inaugurates a genre – advice to a prince – that is central not just to later Greek tradition – Plutarch and Dio Chrysostom, for example, produce famous examples of such work – but also to the Renaissance's discovery of Greek writing (where Machiavelli and Erasmus are probably the most influential exemplars).[71] Isocrates also writes a *Helen*. The opening of this speech is scathing about

---

[70] Isocrates 5. 271–3.
[71] See e.g. Rundle (1998) for an introduction to this vast field.

so-called intellectuals who are mere paradox-mongers, and takes Gorgias to task for calling his speech to Helen an encomium when it is really a defence (*apologia*). His speech will be a real encomium, and he goes on to offer his praise which, he says, will try not to rehearse any of the arguments others have offered. Where Gorgias played so brilliantly with the relation between the power of speech and the reader's critical judgement, Isocrates asks to be judged on his argumentative invention. He is self-assertively dismissive of other styles of oratory and other performers. But as with all of Isocrates' work, this piece also comes under the heading of *didaskalos* and *tekhnikos*: for Isocrates, rhetoric teaches citizens, and is to be taught as a practical discipline. The formalization of the subject has taken place.

   This formalization is most fully instantiated in the work of the greatest of all formalizers, Aristotle. Aristotle calls rhetoric a *hexis*, or 'capability', but unlike Plato, who thought of rhetoric as a dangerous flattery or deception, Aristotle is prepared to argue that it is a *tekhnê*, a discipline, and, as such, open to systematic analysis.[72] Indeed, he claims that his is the first serious comprehensive treatment of rhetoric. Where previous studies, argues Aristotle, had focused almost entirely on how to produce emotional reaction in an audience, his work analyses how an orator ought to construct and present an argument for his conclusions. For Aristotle, rhetoric is part of *politikê* – the science and practice of citizenship and government in the city – and depends for its succees on the performance of the orator in three broad areas of engagement between a speaker and an audience of citizens. First, the argument itself: what forms of evidence, what types of persuasive connection are attempted? It is here that the enthymeme, the argument based on the unstated premise of likelihood or probability is discussed in all its varied types. Second, *êthos*, or the presentation of 'character'. This is where the self-fashioning of the orator as a good and trustworthy citizen is considered. Third, *pathos*, 'emotion': how can an audience's feelings of rage, pity, fear or sympathy be aroused by an orator to support his own case?

   Much of Aristotle's work in the *Rhetoric* is taken up with description of types of argument and with cataloguing types of emotion. He also has many general statements of advice:

---

[72] On Aristotle's *Rhetoric* see the essays collected in Furley and Nehemas edd. (1994); Rorty ed. (1996), which is especially good on 'the emotions', and the briefer general introduction in Wardy (1996), 108–38.

For the purposes of praise or blame, attributes close to reality must be taken as reality: so the cautious man is cold and calculating; or the naive, a good man; the man without feelings, gentle.[73]

Such exaggerations or even distortions are persuasive to most people, explains Aristotle, and useful for constructing expectations: 'If a man risks his life where there is no necessity, how much more would it seem a good idea to him when there is good cause'.[74] But such assertions must take account of the audience: it is difficult if you are speaking before 'Scythians, Spartans or philosophers'[75] – a neatly witty choice of the barbarous, the grimly taciturn, and the dismissively critical! Aristotle creates a systematic matrix of expectations, and empowers the orator and reader to recognize the techniques of persuasiveness. 'The unexamined life is not worth living' was Socrates' maxim (in Plato's words) – a constant injunction to self-reflection and self-consciousness. Aristotle's *Rhetoric* provides a handbook – a map or a guide – for the self-conscious analysis of the central political exchanges of the democratic system.

Rhetoric as a discipline demonstrates an increasing formalization of the techniques of persuasion, and integral to that recognition of the art of speaking well is an increasingly self-conscious reflection on the nature of the performance of speaking and of judging speakers, which is fundamental to democracy in action. Central to rhetoric's self-consciousness is the study of self-presentation: how does the orator construct authority through his character? And how does an orator undermine his opponent's self-fashioning? The ideals of citizenship are thus displayed and staged and manipulated, as these public performances project, explore and worry about what it is to be a subject of democracy – both as speaker and as evaluative audience. Rhetoric, then, should be comprehended broadly as a self-conscious recognition of the role of language in the performance of democracy. The new language of prose – its writing and delivery and interpretation – is absolutely fundamental not just to the intellectual revolution of the fifth-century enlightenment, but also to the political functioning of the classical city.

[73] Arist., *Rhet.* 1. 9. 28–9 (1367a).
[74] Arist., *Rhet.* 1. 9. 30 (1367b).
[75] Arist., *Rhet.* 1. 9. 30 (1367b).

IV. PHILOSOPHY AND SCIENCE:
THE AUTHORITY OF ARGUMENT

Socrates is one of the iconic figures of the classical city – yet he wrote nothing. His teaching consisted in conversations with the people he met (we are told), particularly in the very highest circles of the cultivated and the powerful. He was prosecuted and put to death – and his execution has become the paradigmatic image of the man of principle standing firmly and calmly by his principles to the point of death, an image that Christian martyrology learnt a lot from. Socrates, however, is written about by many. He appears on the comic stage of Aristophanes as a leading sophist, he is memorialized by his followers, for example by Xenophon in his *Memorabilia, Apology* and *Oikonomikos*, and in particular he is the leading figure in the dialogues of Plato.[1] It is first with Plato's massive contribution to the invention of prose that this chapter is concerned.

The point of starting with Socrates is to mark once again how a deep-seated love of irony and paradox courses through this history of prose. Socrates not only wrote nothing, but, in Plato's prose, is made to denigrate writing altogether. The trouble with books, says Socrates in the *Phaedrus*, is that they never answer back. When you put a question to them to gain knowledge, books can only say the same thing. They run around the world without proper authority – there is no *patêr logou*, no 'father of the discourse', to take responsibility for what is said or to protect it. When the Egyptian Theuth invented writing it should just have been given back to the inventor with a firm 'no, thank you'.[2] A philosopher writing that writing is untrustworthy and inappropriate for philosophy is not so far from Gorgias telling you rather clearly that 'if anything exists, it can't be apprehended, and if man can apprehend it, he can't communicate it'. What's more, where Thucydides and Herodotus both insisted on the authority of presence – the eyewitness who sees – Plato almost never enters his own texts, and when he does it is to say he *wasn't* present. Thus at the famous death-bed scene of Socrates in prison, Plato lists Socrates' grieving friends who make up the chorus to Socrates' heroic end, only to add 'but Plato was ill' – and thus was not

---

[1] On the non-Platonic treatments see Vander Waerdt ed. (1994); Kahn (1995), 1–35.
[2] *Phaedrus* 274c3–276e5: see Ferrari (1987); Derrida (1981), 61–172.

there.[3] Plato may dismiss rhetoric and sophistry as mere word games, but this is certainly not because his prose is austere, scientific, and rigorously argued logic. When you add that Socrates, his leading character, is a master of irony, it will become clear that you must be extremely cautious about reading Plato's prose too quickly. Not only do dialogues inevitably set up a drama of different voices, but Plato also loves to play involuted games of voices within voices, all presided over by the questioning irony of Socrates.[4]

Yet one strategy of Plato is constant. Plato never stops working to establish philosophy as the authoritative intellectual and educational discipline. It is not clear if Plato invented the word 'philosophy', but he is certainly instrumental in philosophy emerging as a recognizable practice or subject.[5] On the one hand, Plato defines and defends philosophy as the only intellectual activity which aims absolutely at truth and goodness, and which scrutinizes itself with enough rigour to maintain that focus on truth and goodness. On the other hand, all the other disciplines are ruthlessly criticized, denigrated, and eventually banned from the ideal city of philosophy. So, rhetoric and sophistry are humiliated in dialogues like *Gorgias*, the *Sophist*, *Protagoras*, *Phaedrus*. Tragedy is explored and banished in the *Republic*; Homer is represented by the slow-witted bard Ion in the *Ion*, and carefully sidelined in the *Republic*. The Funeral Oration over the War Dead may stand for the political rhetoric of Athens: in *Menexenus* Socrates recites a parodic version of such a speech written, he claims, by the courtesan Aspasia, Pericles' mistress. Politicians are shown up as either ineffectual and foolish (*Laches*) or as flatterers trying to tame the dangerous beast of The Public (*Republic*). All this despite – or perhaps because of – the fact that Plato speaks of the attraction and power of Homer and tragedy with real feeling, and has Socrates argue with all the outrageous panache of the market-place when it suits, and has a strong political agenda from the beginning to the end of his writing career. For Plato, philosophy must take the high ground and keep it.

In the *Apology*, Socrates describes how the Delphic oracle announced that he was the wisest [*sophôtatos*] of men. Unwilling to accept such an oracle, he visited politicians, poets and artisans, and, in each case, when he questions the men who appeared to have authoritative knowledge

---

[3] See Press ed. (2000) for the most recent discussions – though the quality of the essays is very varied.

[4] See Nehamas (1998); Griswold ed. (1988); Nightingale (1995); Vlastos (1991).

[5] The most strident arguments are around Schiappa (1990) and (1999).

[*sophia*], he found that they knew very little indeed. Socrates concludes that he is the wisest in that he knows he is ignorant. This is a paradigmatic scene. On the one hand, we see the philosopher declare with complete self-serving authority that his *sophia* – philosophy – is the only discipline that deserves the title of knowledge; all others with claims to authoritative wisdom are charlatans. On the other hand, the story is told with a particularly complex self-deprecating irony. It is not just that Socrates depicts himself as ignorant, and bumbling around finding out the ignorance of others by mistake (as it were), in the course of trying to show that others really are wiser than he is. Rather, the irony also stems from the fact that we know that this defence speech fails. Socrates is found guilty and condemned to death by the jury. Several versions of Socrates' self-defence circulated and none can be given priority: we just don't know what Socrates actually said in court.[6] What's more difficult to judge is whether Plato has given Socrates here a speech guaranteed to alienate an audience of citizens (thus explaining his conviction) or whether he has given Socrates the sort of winning speech he should have made (exculpating his master)? Or is it carefully balanced to persuade the philosopher or posterity (while being misjudged enough to show why he was executed)? Or is it designed to turn a citizen audience towards shame and regret for their decision? Plato thus constantly promotes the privilege of philosophy – but it is rarely simple and never naive propaganda for his discipline.

So what are the special claims that Plato makes for philosophy? Is philosophical prose – philosophical practice – different from the other writing I have been considering? We shall see in the third section of this chapter how Plato argues that philosophy defines the relationship between *logos* and truth differently from other disciplines, and also defines the relationship between the philosopher and his self-understanding, and between the philosopher and other people, in a special way. The unwavering pursuit of truth through logical argument is a basic element of philosophy's self-image. And there is an easily told historical account that travels from Socrates on a street corner, to Plato's institutionalization of the discipline (crowned with the foundation of the Academy, his philosophy school which still attracted the best and brightest hundreds of years later in the Roman Empire), and then to Aristotle who not only founds his own school, the Lyceum, but who also systematizes logic and metaphysics into formal branches of a science –

[6] See Brickhouse and Smith (1989); Stone (1988).

which continues into the philosophy degrees of today's universities. It would be foolish to deny that Aristotle's treatises on logic mark a significant development in form and method from a Socratic conversation, even as reported by Plato. Yet, it is important also to be careful not to read Plato with a perspective formulated too strongly from the later institutionalization of philosophy. For Plato's writing offers an extraordinary richness of expressive modes and persuasive techniques, which go far beyond later definitions of philosophical technique.

Take the *Symposium*, for example, one of the dialogues read throughout antiquity and of huge influence in Western thinking on love and desire.[7] The *Symposium* is (technically) a dialogue between one Apollodorus and an unnamed companion. Apollodorus tells his friend that on the previous day he had met another friend, Glaukon, who had heard that Apollodorus knew the story of a party at which Agathon, Socrates and others had talked of desire [*erôs*]. Apollodorus agrees to tell him the story which he heard (he tells us) from Aristodemus. The version Glaukon had heard was muddled, and now it will be put right. Hearing this, the unnamed companion asks to hear the story too – and Apollodorus tells it (again). So the *Symposium* is set up as a repeated conversation where one man (Apollodorus) tells another the story he heard from Aristodemus, of a conversation many years ago (and sometimes muddled). What's more, in this account – all given in reported speech, of course – Socrates gives a long speech in which he recalls a conversation he had many years before with a priestess called Diotima, who tells him about the nature of desire – a story which, Socrates is quick to tell his companions, he believes.[8]

No Thucydidean eye-witness here, then, no logical treatise! The recession of voices, like Russian dolls, constantly sets the truth of love as a distant thing. Diotima tells Socrates that desire may start as a longing for a beautiful body but it moves on first to longing for a beautiful soul and finally to seek after the beautiful itself. To see and be with beauty itself is the ultimate goal of desire. Diotima's story is of a series of stages of longing to be with something distant – as her story is itself set in this nesting of fading voices, in pursuit of the Real Thing.

The participants in this drinking party seem to represent a cross-section of experts in those fields which might be thought to be authoritative about *erôs*. The speakers, each of whom is to praise

---

[7] See Nussbaum (1986), 165–99; Halperin (1992); Price (1989); Gagarin (1977); Penwill (1978), each with lengthy bibliographies.
[8] See Halperin (1990), 113–51, with plenty of further bibliography; also Henderson (2000).

desire, include Phaedrus (who appears in the dialogue *Phaedrus*, which is also about desire): his speech is a cultivated and literary reflection on Eros as a god in myth and cult, that is, a religious and traditional version. Pausanias, Agathon's lover (and thus experienced in *erôs*) introduces the distinction between *Aphroditê Ouranios*, 'Heavenly Aphrodite', and *Aphroditê Pandêmios*, 'Aphrodite of the People'. These rather grand terms distinguish between mere physical gratification, that is, desire interested in sexual satisfaction, and desire which has the noble aim of the beloved's soul. This dualism has not just an evident moralism, but also a socio-political aspect in its defence of a particular educational and traditionally aristocratic model of male erotic relations with younger males. Eryximachus, the doctor, speaks next, and he extends Pausanias' distinction into a sort of principle of nature: opposites like wet and dry must reconcile each other, and, as a doctor, it is is his job to help implant healthy – balanced – *erôs*. There is a physics as well as a metaphysics of desire which the doctor sets on the agenda. Aristophanes, the comic playwright, produces a brilliant comic myth (in line with the greatest fantasies of his drama). He imagines a world where humans used to be strange four-legged, two-headed creatures. Zeus split these figures in two, and now everyone wanders around looking for his/her other half – and when this other half is found, desires to be rejoined together. Agathon, the tragic poet, speaks next and he gives a finely lyrical and highly poetical encomium of the god in the most high-flown of language.

Thus the five speakers represent varied authoritative discourses of the city on desire. Who speaks best of love? The comedian? The tragedian? The doctor? The sophisticated lover? The world of religion and tradition? The dialogue is thus set up for philosophy – Socrates – to trump them all with his remarkable account of Diotima's education into philosophical passion, the desire to find the good in man's soul and nourish it. And no doubt Socrates' speech is climactic. Yet the moment he has finished speaking, there is a crashing noise from the courtyard, and in bursts Alcibiades, the most charismatic young man of Athens, drunk, garlanded, supported by a couple of flute-girls. This wonderfully wild irruption of the most disreputable and fascinating figure changes the direction of the dialogue. For the framing of the dialogue makes quite clear the difference between the historical setting of the drinking party and the time of its retelling. At the time of the drinking party, Alcibiades is young, attractive, rich and exuberant. At the time of the retelling, Alcibiades has been branded a traitor, been instrumental in Athenian military disaster and defeat, returned from exile in triumph, been exiled again and assassinated in Persia. Socrates, too, has been put to death for corrupting the young. This gives the exchanges between Socrates and Alcibiades in the *Symposium* an extraordinary charge – especially since Alcibiades tells the shocking tale of how he tried to seduce Socrates. Alcibiades, joining the party, relates a very different type of erotic story from the earlier speeches.

For Alcibiades praises Socrates – as the object of his desire. He begins with a set of images for how Socrates works on him. Socrates, he says, is like a doll of a Silenus (a satyr): the Silenus is ugly, of course, with a pot-belly and snub nose (like the standard images of Socrates), but when you open the doll, inside are lovely statues of the gods. So, Socrates is ugly on the outside and nobly beautiful on the inside. In Greek culture in general, external form is taken as a sign of internal worth: the greatest hero Achilles is the most beautiful, and the worst man at Troy, Thersites, is humpbacked, pigeon-chested and bald.[9] Socrates reverses this model: what counts now is an internal life which has no necessary relation to outward signs of class, birth or wealth. (Again, the importance of Socrates for Christianity is evident.) 'He regards all these possessions as worthless and us too – I am speaking to you; he spends all his life being ironic and joking at humans. When he is serious and opened up, I don't know if anyone has seen those statues inside. But I saw them once, and they seemed to me to be so divine and golden and beauteous and amazing that I had to do, in short, whatever Socrates ordered'.[10] The glimpse of the true Socrates, the inside, leads Alcibiades to desire Socrates.

So, Alcibiades goes on to explain how he became desperate for Socrates' company and to learn from him. He invited him to dinner; they worked out together; he invited him to a party, just the two of them; he persuaded Socrates to stay the night, in the same room; and then tried to get Socrates to be his lover: 'I shoved him and said, "Socrates, are you asleep?". "No", he said. "Do you know what I think?" "What?' he said. "You seem to me to be the only man worthy to be my lover . . .".'[11] Socrates, however, with gentle irony avoids the young man's come-on, leaving Alcibiades – as he describes it – 'mocked and humiliated'. It is quite against the norms of Greek courtship for the young man to be so forward (although it certainly helps characterize the transgressive

---

[9] On Thersites see Thalmann (1988); in general on the body and worth, see Foucault (1987); Vernant (1991), 50–75; Stewart (1997).

[10] Plato, *Symp.* 216e2–217a1.

[11] Plato, *Symp.* 218b8–c7.

Alcibiades); he is still sufficiently forward (or drunk) to describe his outrageous behaviour and Socrates' rebuff. This is a very striking image indeed, as the ugly Socrates rejects the improper advances of the most desirable young man. It both represents Alcibiades as marked out for his future life of outrage, and separates Socrates from any sign of active corruption.[12]

Alcibiades goes on to praise Socrates for his self-control and sobriety in other areas too, and the party gradually sinks into the closure of drunken oblivion, with Socrates still talking till everyone passes out. Then he goes back to the Lyceum for a bath, ready to start another day's philosophizing.

This bursting on to the scene by Alcibiades has two crucial effects on the dialogue. First, the praise of *erôs* turns into praise of Socrates, praise which emphasizes the philosopher's preternatural self-control when it comes to sex, drink and material comforts, as it emphasizes the attractiveness of his speech and personality. It demonstrates how far Socrates is from 'corrupting the youth'. It shows him trying – though failing – to lead the dangerous golden boy of Athenian politics towards the good by abstinence, self-control and education. This is, in short, apologetics for Socrates – a defence of the master, not by argumentation as in the *Apology* but by the representation of his behaviour and character as reported by one of the so-called 'corrupted youths'.

Second, however, we must also ask what difference the entrance of Alcibiades makes to our understanding of Socrates' speech.[13] Socrates has just delivered his version of a non-physical, spiritual yearning for the good itself. Alcibiades then enters with his very different erotic adventure story. It might be thought that Socrates' behaviour fully instantiates the ideals of Diotima's image of a philosopher's desire. After all, he resists the physical charms of Alcibiades and remains focused on the good. But it might be thought that Alcibiades' entrance is slightly more ironizing.[14] The all too physical gestures of Alcibiades show up a misplaced idealism: how does a philosopher's desire for the good itself actually relate to working out together and sleeping under the same blanket? And if this is Socrates' desire at work, isn't it rather worrying that the result is the continuing outrageousness of Alcibiades? Can the ideal of 'contemplating the beautiful itself' be anything other than a

[12] For the protocols of male desire, see Dover (1978), Foucault (1987) and Winkler (1990); for the scene here see also Nussbaum (1986), 165–99; Gagarin (1977); Nehamas (1998), 60–9.
[13] See Nussbaum (1986), 165–99; Gagarin (1977).
[14] So Nussbaum (1986), provocatively.

unobtainable ideal, a fantasy? Or is Socrates the first in Greek myth to resist *erôs* successfully? Now, as these questions indicate, different readers have put together Socrates' speech and Alcibiades' sexual story in different ways. What is important for my argument here, however, is not to evaluate these varied attempts to deal with this interpretative drama. What counts here is that the argument of the dialogue proceeds by *juxtaposition*, not by logical discussion (or any other style of standard philosophical process). It is the juxtaposition of Socrates' speech to Alcibiades' performance which raises a question – which the dialogue leaves to the reader to answer, much as the audience of a play watches a debate, or the citizens in the Assembly decide between proposals.

The *Symposium*, then, constructs a series of frames in which the pursuit of *erôs* turns into the pursuit of the lost voice of Socrates, the concealed gods within. Aristodemus – with typical Platonic wit – confesses that at the end he nodded off and missed what Socrates was on about: Socrates' voice (in Aristodemus' account recalled by Apollodorus written by Plato) fades out . . . The dialogue makes an erotic hero of Socrates – while leaving his own ideal account of desire in juxtaposition to Alcibiades' more earthy understandings. The *Symposium* is so sophisticated and so rich in the manner in which it creates its meanings that it proves extremely difficult to fit it into philosophy's own description of its practices.

The *Symposium*'s intricate layering of different voices is particularly complex and engaging. Is there not a more direct access to the voice of Socrates – or at least to the voice of Plato's Socrates? The *Charmides* is a piece written in the first-person voice.[15] The only speaker is Socrates:

On the evening of the previous day, we got back from the camp at Potidaia, and I was delighted after such an absence to go to my usual hangouts. So I went down to Taureas' gym, opposite the temple of the Queen.[16]

The historical and geographical setting could scarcely be more precise, more immediate. The battle of Potidaia took place in 432 BCE – Socrates and Alcibiades both fought, and in the *Symposium* Alcibiades describes Socrates' bravery and bare-footed hardiness.[17] There were some fine epigrams set up by the city to record the Athenian

---

[15] On *Charmides* see von Reden and Goldhill (1999); McKim (1985); Kahn (1995), 163–209; and, for extensive bibliography to philosophical treatments, Schmid (1998).

[16] Plato, *Charmides* 153a1–4.

[17] Plato, *Symp.* 219d3–221c1.

losses. The gym, Socrates' regular hangout, is given a name and an address. We know where we are in this dialogue. The first-person voice, along with such precision, gives a strong sense of immediacy – an effect of reality. Yet it cannot be forgotten that here we have Plato, writing at least forty years after the event, ventriloquizing the voice of his master, offering us Socrates' inner thoughts as the dialogue progresses. Is this looking inside Socrates, as Alcibiades hoped to do? Seeing the real Socrates? Does Socrates' irony become clear, now it is in the first person?[18] These questions are particularly pointed as the dialogue progresses. For Socrates asks Critias – the future murderous tyrant – if there is anyone around who is particularly distinguished in philosophy or beauty – a typical Socratic pairing! – and Critias tells him to look at the door, because the beauty of the moment, Charmides, is about to enter. Here is Socrates' response:

Now, I am, my friend, no connoisseur. I am simply a ruler without lines when it comes to beautiful guys – almost everyone of the right age looks beautiful to me in some way; but that boy at that time seemed quite amazing for his beauty and physical presence. Everyone else seemed to desire him – they were so struck and confused when he came in – and many others followed in his train.[19]

This is a marvellous description of the effect of a beauty's grand entrance into the gym. But how ironical is Socrates to be taken to be, as he confesses to us, the readers ('my friend'), that he really is just a fool for any young man – or when he describes the overwhelming effects of the boy on everyone on the gym? Charmides is called over and sits between Socrates and Critias:

He gave me such a look with his eyes as passes description, and was just about to ask his question; but all the people in the gym surged around us in a circle, and at that point I saw inside his cloak, and caught fire, and I was no longer inside myself, and I thought Cydias the poet was the wisest in love matters when he said – talking of a beautiful boy and giving advice to someone – 'Beware of coming as a fawn before a lion and being seized as his portion of flesh'. I too felt I had been grabbed by such a beast.[20]

Socrates catches a glimpse under Charmides' cloak and sees his body – and is racked by desire. He is no longer 'inside himself' – and now finds a poet to be wisest [*sophôtatos*] in erotic matters. This, of course, is the

---

[18] It is extraordinary – but typical of many philosophers' responses to Plato's writing – that Charles Kahn's lengthy treatment of 'self-knowledge' in the *Charmides* fails to mention that it is a first-person fictional narrative – even when he asks (Kahn (1996), 200): 'How can one *know* what someone else knows or does not know?'!

[19] Plato, *Charmides* 154b7–c5.

[20] Plato, *Charmides* 155c8–e1.

Socrates who went to the poets and rejected them as *sophos* in the *Apology*, and who held forth as an authority on *erôs* in the *Symposium*. When desire makes him not himself, he falls back on poetic wisdom like any stereotypic lover (with what irony for the philosopher?).

Socrates will flirt with the boy, but no more. As the group of men in the gym crowd round rather ridiculously, a double audience is created. On the one hand, his conversation takes place in front of a group of citizens who see him discussing self-control [*sôphrosunê*] and displaying it in his restraint towards Charmides. It is equally important that Critias, the future tyrant, is one of those in this audience. He is shown to watch a lesson in self-control which he will spectacularly fail to learn from. On the other hand, the reader is given special access to the internal struggle of Socrates as he struggles to maintain that self-control – access which is not unmediated, but always open to Socratic irony, especially when he seems to address the reader. It should be clear that once again Plato's apologetic agenda is at work: not only does Socrates not act corruptly towards the sexy youth, but also he tries to lead the future tyrant towards a better understanding of good citizenship. The argument about self-control is not an abstract, logical discussion, but a conversation between a desiring man and a pretty boy, contextualized not just in the erotic space of the gym, but also with an audience of admiring men, among them the future tyrant; and with the added layer of a first-person commentary, a commentary from an ironist, which addresses the reader. It would seem that the first-person voice constructs as complex a scene of performance as the multilayered narrative of the *Symposium*.

Where Herodotus and Thucydides use the first-person mode to give authority to their writing by adopting the role of the eye-witness or the critical interpreter, Plato writes as Socrates – and this theatricality produces a vividly dramatic scene, but plays a very knowing game with the desire to have unmediated access to Socrates' meaning. Lysias writes a speech for Euphiletus to deliver, in the first person: he produces a script for self-presentation. Plato, however, writes as if he opens up Socrates to us, an intimate, personal communication. Plato often describes how Socrates' followers wanted desperately to spend time with Socrates to find out what he knows. (We have seen Alcibiades in the *Symposium* report such a reaction.) The first-person voice here seems to offer the reader such intimate time with Socrates – while the 'as if' of Plato's dramatic writing constantly leaves the reader barred from such an exchange. Plato's first-person writing is luring the reader into engaging in the engrossing conversation of philosophy.

Plato's persuasiveness is nowhere more evident than in his skill at what is called in rhetoric *êthopoeia*, 'the construction of character'. The final scenes of Socrates' life as portrayed in the *Phaedo* in particular are central to the image of Socrates that has been passed on to later generations.[21] On his last night, Socrates dismisses his weeping wife, in order to spend time discussing the immortality of the soul. As the hour of execution approaches, his friends become more distraught and Socrates becomes even calmer, as he tries in different ways to persuade his companions that the soul is immortal and thus death is not to be feared. He drinks the hemlock with a brief final quip. Socrates' commitment to an ethical life, tested by argument, is *performed* rather than argued for. Socrates becomes an example to live by. Similarly, his refusal to escape from his prison cell when offered the chance, because of his obligation to the law, is impressive not necessarily for the arguments he offers Crito, his potential benefactor, but for the seriousness of his commitment to an ethical position in the face of such a punishment and such a promise of escape.[22] The incorruptible, hardy, ironical, ethically and politically committed Socrates – the image that dominates Western ideas of philosophy – is Plato's invention. Plato may attack the psychology and persuasive techniques of tragic theatre and rhetoric, but his own prose similarly sets out to persuade through emotional manipulation, dramatic characterization, and wonderfully evocative 'reality effects'. Plato repeatedly claims a special status for philosophy as a discipline, and for philosophical prose as a form of argument – but he also brilliantly appropriates the power and strategies of the other forms of prose I have been discussing in this book.

II

What, then, distinguishes the prose of the philosopher?

The first element I wish to emphasize looks back to the legal and political forums of democracy, and is known usually as *elenchus*, which means a cross-examination or testing, commonly with the purpose of refutation. (This is by no means an exclusively or specifically democratic procedure, though it certainly plays a large role in the democratic city.) Opponents may be brought forth in a trial for cross-examination

---

[21] For different responses to that heritage see e.g. Nehemas (1998) (Montaigne to Nietzsche) and Zanker (1995) (later intellectual types of antiquity).

[22] See Kraut (1984) and, most recently, Weiss (1998).

(as we saw above in Lysias' *Against Eratosthenes*), and all officials of democracy were subject to scrutiny [*euthunai*] as a very sign of democratic accountability. But in the hands of Socrates and Plato, *elenchus* becomes a privileged philosophical strategy.[23] Since I have been discussing the construction of authority, it is worth saying from the outset that *elenchus* is used primarily to challenge the authority of others and, in so doing, implicitly to build up the authority of the philosopher. *Elenchus* is the archetypal strategy of the figure who claims he is wise only because he knows that he knows nothing – and can *show* that those who think they know are really ignorant.

The *Charmides* offers a good example of the *elenchus* in action – and will allow us to see how the dialogue moves into more detailed argument from its rather chatty and sexy beginning.[24] Socrates wants Charmides to tell him what *sôphrosunê* – the quality I have been translating 'self-control' – means. Its sense ranges from sexual chastity through social propriety to political moderation, but Socrates is seeking a definition. Charmides with some prompting suggests 'to do everything in an orderly [*kosmiôs*] and calm [*hêsukhiêi*] manner'. Socrates leaps in: 'Okay, they do say, Charmides, that the calm are self-controlled. Let's see if that holds water. Tell me, is self-control not a good thing?' Charmides agrees. 'So,' continues Socrates, 'is it best in writing school to write the same letters quickly or calmly?' 'Quickly.' 'What about reading? Quickly or slowly?' 'Quickly' . . . and so on, as Socrates, taking calmness as slowness, easily demonstrates that in many activities speed is what is valued as a good thing and not to be at rest, to be 'calm' [*hêsukhos*]. 'It is better to learn quickly than slowly and calmly.'[25] The first attempt at a definition is progressively refuted by a process of question and answer.

The *Charmides* goes on to try five further definitions of progressively more complexity. Is it *aidôs* ('shame', 'reverence')? Attending to one's own business? (Those two offerings are also by Charmides, and equally quickly dismissed.) Then Critias takes over ('in a spirit of competitive rivalry'[26]) and suggests 'self-knowledge'. This is then developed into 'knowledge which knows other knowledges and itself' and finally 'knowledge of what one knows and does not know' – which is indeed getting close to Socrates' self-description in the *Apology*. Socrates

---

[23] Good introduction to this in Vlastos (1994), 1–37.
[24] See Schmid (1998).
[25] Plato, *Charmides* 159b7–160d2.
[26] Plato, *Charmides* 162c1.

concludes: 'Now we have been defeated on all sides, and we cannot discover on what aspect of reality the lawgiver set that name *sôphrosunê*.[27] The process of definition goes through six attempts and finally ends in *aporia* – systematic doubt. This conclusion in uncertainty is common particular in what are known as the early dialogues.[28] So the *Lysis* – another dialogue involving handsome youths and much flirtation in the gym – discusses what friendship [*philia*] is, and concludes, as the boys are called off home by their personal trainers, with Socrates' final comment:

'Well now, Lysis and Menexenus,' I said, 'we have proved ourselves a laughing-stock, you and I, an old man. For this lot will go away and say that we think we are friends of one another – for I count myself in your team – but we haven't been able yet to discover what a friend is!'[29]

With much irony, the old man who hangs around with beautiful young men, notes that they are all now friends, and have become friends through their discussion – but that they can't define the word. There is a significant tension here between the flirtatious male bonding and the attempt to define friendship rigorously, much as the failure to define *sôphrosunê* in the *Charmides* is tellingly conducted between Socrates and a young beauty, *and* between Socrates and a future tyrant.[30]

The move to definition through the refutation of *elenchus* is, however, certainly not always destined to end in doubt [*aporia*]. The whole of the *Republic*, Plato's lengthy description of an ideal state, is the search to define what is a just city, which begins in elenchtic style by rejecting the commonplace of traditional thought that justice consists in doing good to one's friends and harm to one's enemies; and second by throwing out the commonplace of contemporary sophistic thought, that might is right – justice is what benefits the powerful. This last position is proposed by Thrasymachus, and not only does Plato characterize him as personally aggressive and blustering, but also he has Socrates take some pleasure in reducing him to blushing confusion. This great work of political theory also mobilizes *êthopoeia* to good effect.[31]

---

[27] Plato, *Charmides* 175b2–4.
[28] The dating of Plato's dialogues is extremely contentious, however, and always tied up with ideas of the 'development' (or lack of development) within the Platonic corpus: that Plato's dialogues refer to each other does indicate an important idea for the history of prose: that different prose works of an author could/should be considered *as* parts of a corpus. Nothing in my argument here depends on the date of the *Lysis* or the *Charmides*.
[29] Plato, *Lysis* 223b3–9.
[30] See von Reden and Goldhill (1999), with bibliography.
[31] See for an introduction to the *Republic* Annas (1981).

Elenchus, then, is the argumentative instantiation of the Socratic principle that 'the unexamined life is not worth living'. *Elenchus* is the examination of the values of life in process.

The process of question, answer, qualification, requestioning and so on is basic to Platonic prose. It is the grounding of the most basic of all the problems in studying Plato: why doesn't Plato write treatises? Why doesn't he express any doctrines or views in his own voice or name? Why does philosophy begin with *dialogue*? My setting of Plato here in the context of the invention of prose – the cultural revolution of the classical *polis* – should have made one aspect of this issue clear, namely, how closely involved Plato's prose is with the other genres of writing I have been discussing.[32] The democratic requirement of hearing both sides of a question, the need to stage public debate, fundamental to the democratic system, have an impact on every writer of the fifth and fourth century, from tragedy to Thucydides to the rhetorician's self-assertivenes. In composing dialogues Plato is not only attempting to capture the practice of Socrates himself, but also setting himself within the scene of Athenian democratic exchange (whatever his own political views).[33] Looking back at Plato from the later development of philosophy inevitably prompts the question 'Why dialogue?'[34] Looking at Plato within his contemporary context, it is perhaps easier to see how he has worked out a particular individual position for himself, adapting and adopting the *êthopoeia* of the orators, the analytic and dramatic flair of a Thucydides, the explanatory and revelatory dialogue of tragedy, and the cut and thrust of sophistic exchange, while resisting the expository pamphleteering of Isocrates and the epideictic display of the professional orator.

Above all, however, Plato's unique development of the ideal of free exchange of ideas between citizens projects a remarkable and highly complex sense of *authority* – which produces a dizzying set of tensions. Dialogue allows for a play of voices – yet Socrates is usually dominant. So does Socrates speak for Plato, his author? Or does the representation of Socrates allow Plato also to show up bad or manipulative arguments in his master's voice – for the reader to evaluate and learn from? Does

---

[32] See in particular Nightingale (1995).

[33] This is the starting point of both Saxenhouse (1992) and Monoson (2000), though neither is wholly convincing in the full range of their arguments. Gouldner (1965) is still valuable. Gill (1995) puts such a development within 'Greek Thought'.

[34] Many answers of varying types and convincingness: see e.g. Kahn (1983); the contributors to Griswold ed. (1988), especially Desjardins and Griswold; Coventry (1990); Sayre (1995); Press ed. (1993).

Socrates represent Plato's view, or are Plato's real ideas always else-where? The arguments repeatedly move towards the most abstract terms: the good itself, justice as a priniciple. Yet, again and again, arguments are directed at particular individuals and manipulate their characters, their flaws, their understandings. The contexts and peculiar-ities of dialogue provoke the question of how generalizable and how particular this philosophical argument is to be. Socrates is undoubtedly an authority figure – yet he repeatedly uses his irony to refuse such authority. Indeed, one of the most difficult and dynamic tensions in Plato's writing is the fact that this dialogic and ironic style works towards the political system argued for in the *Republic* (and the *Laws*), which seems so deeply *authoritarian*, with each aspect of life controlled and ordered by philosopher-kings whose knowledge gives them power and authority to legislate and regulate the details and the totality of a city's functioning. And to lie to the citizens in the name of such social order. Is dialogue's pleasurably ironic openness a misleading lure towards an authoritarian vision, where one can only say 'yes' to authority?

These tensions have provoked some of the most heated recent discussion of Plato – and once again show that to discuss the invention of prose is inevitably to become embroiled in the issue of how authority is formulated and expressed in writing.[35]

So far I have looked primarily at *elenchus* as a technique of refutation. Yet Plato develops 'conversation' into further technical philosophical strategies that have a more positive and constructive aim and outcome. The *Meno* is about what virtue is and whether it can be taught (one of the central questions of contemporary intellectual debate, as we have seen).[36] After facing some elenchtic challenging from Socrates on his views of what virtue is, Meno proposes a paradox (which echoes Gorgias' style): 'How can you enquire into something, if you don't know what it is? Which of the things that you don't know will you suppose it to be, when you are enquiring into it? And even if you happen upon it, how will you know it is the thing you didn't know?' So – as Socrates reformulates it – 'if you don't know what virtue is, you cannot study it. If you do know what virtue is, what's to study?'[37] I am not concerned to analyse the strength of this paradoxical argument, so much

---

[35] See e.g. Vlastos (1991); Nightingale (1995); Nehemas (1998); Nehemas (1999); Monoson (2000).

[36] On the *Meno* see especially Day (1994); Weiss (2001) and, more generally, Scott (1995). Good brief introduction in Fine (1992) and Nehemas (1999), 3–26.

[37] Plato, *Meno* 80d5–e5.

as to look at Socrates' response which, in part at least, is to propose the theory of 'recollection' [*anamnêsis*], that is, that coming to learn is a form of remembering.[38] One demonstration of this is a lesson whereby Socrates teaches a slave some basic geometry which he didn't know earlier.[39] Socrates asks the boy if he knows what a square is. The boy says 'yes' (as he will to many of the questions to come). He gets the boy to demonstrate that a two-foot by two-foot square has an area of four square feet. 'What, then,' asks Socrates, 'will be the area of a square if we double the length of each side of the square?' 'Eight,' replies the boy. Socrates then underlines for Meno that the boy thinks that he knows the answer. He proceeds to disabuse him, by drawing a square with each side twice the length of the two foot square:

Soc: Does this not give us what you said was an eight square foot shape?
Boy: Yes.
Soc: How big is it, then? Aren't there four squares the size of the first?
Boy: Of course.
Soc: Is the four-foot square double the size of the first one?
Boy: No, by God.
Soc: How big, then?
Boy: Four times.
Soc: So, then, doubling the sides has not produced a double but a four-fold area?
Boy: You speak the truth.[40]

Here, question and answer proceed from a hypothesis, via empirical testing, to a refined conclusion. 'You speak the truth,' concludes the boy aptly. This has been an authoritative display by Socrates, moving with unerring concision from a false assumption, via investigation, to an accurate and precise conclusion. Unlike the destructive *elenchus*, the boy's education is simple and direct. It is part of the questioning of Meno, of course, and has a role to play in the broader questions of the dialogue. None the less, this passage also shows philosophy using dialogue to draw close to a scientific or mathematical model of hypothesis testing. Philosophy seems to appropriate for itself the authority of rigorous, demonstrable proof. Hence, the love of the syllogism and the formalization of the syllogism which I will discuss in the next section of the chapter.

Plato indeed develops a special principle of 'conversation aimed at

---

[38] See Fine (1992); Nehemas (1999), 3–26; Day (1994); Weiss (2001) and, more generally, Scott (1995).

[39] Plato, *Meno* 82b8–85b7.

[40] Plato, *Meno* 83b1–c1.

discovering the truth', which he calls 'dialectic' (from *dialegesthai*, 'to have a conversation'). He distinguishes this procedure from point-scoring and arguments aimed just at winning (the sophist and the rhetorician) – though philosophers ever since have disagreed considerably about exactly how Plato conceives of this distinction, and what formal properties 'dialectic' has.[41] Dialectic demands of its participants a commitment to a shared enterprise of moving together through careful, evaluative argument towards an agreed conclusion. It requires not just a procedure or a methodology, but also a shared social and intellectual commitment to a form of exchange. Dialectic is to make philosophers of us all. That, perhaps, is the one overriding reason why dialogue is the medium for Plato's philosophy. The act of performing dialogue by reading it encourages an enactment that aims to draw the reader towards the ideals of dialectic – the ideals of doing Platonic philosophy. Plato wants his dialogues to *engage* you.

Plato has a simple catchphrase for what it would mean for a person's view to be authoritative. It is the ability *logon didonai*, 'to give an account'. By this, Plato means not just having a true belief about something which you can communicate; nor indeed being able to declare that such and such a thing is true (when it is). Rather, he means being able to give a systematic account, which is explanatory and which is open to testing and which after testing can be demonstrated to be the case. The outcome of this Plato calls *epistêmê*, which can be translated 'knowledge' or 'science'. Its root meaning is 'knowing (how)'; but in Plato's hands, it implies a disciplinary or systematic knowledge, a knowledge which is privileged as true knowledge. Sometimes he calls this process of the production of knowledge *logismos aitias*, 'the calculation of cause/reason': where Thucydides and Herodotus pursue the *aitia* of war, or Lysias places *aitia* in the frame of the courtroom, Plato seeks to make knowledge dependent on the process of rationally evaluating and systematizing cause/reason. Now, I do not wish to pretend to involve myself here in the heady world of Plato's theories of knowledge.[42] What I want to emphasize rather is Plato's appropriation of the rather simple phrase *logon didonai*, 'to give an account', 'to produce a *logos*'. Any one of the writers I have discussed so far in this book could describe all or part of their work as the production of *logos*. *Logos* is normal Greek, after all, for a 'speech', a 'tale', a 'story', an 'account', a 'rationale'. Democracy, in Demosthenes' words, is a constitution of

---

[41] See Robinson (1953); Mueller (1992); Gonzalez (1998); Nehemas (1999), 108–22.
[42] Burnyeat (1990) is a great if taxingly difficult start.

logoi. What Plato sets out to do is to give a special meaning to the idea of *logon didonai*, to circumscribe *logos* by the practice and ideals of his philosophy. That 'logic', the branch of thinking pertaining to *logos*, should become the name for philosophy's special area indicates the success of Plato's appropriation. It is around this word, *logos*, that the *contest* over authority instantiated in the invention of prose is most strikingly acted out.

It should be clear that I have not tried to give an account here of Platonic philosophy in the sense of the content of his arguments, doctrines or beliefs. What I have attempted to show rather is how Plato's dialogues first of all develop a series of techniques and concerns that are deeply rooted in the cultural milieu in which they were produced. Dialogue itself is integral to democratic practice at an institutional and theoretical level. The persuasive representation of character through such exchange is basic to drama and to the law-court. The dramatic staging of competing views is part and parcel of the Assembly. Seeing two sides to each question and moving through such debate to public decision is the essence of democratic political activity. Yet Plato develops such elements into an extraordinarily complex and unique form. Central to this is the representation of Socrates, and Plato's veiling of his own voice. Plato writes dialogue in another's voice at another time. This leads in the *Symposium* to the most intricate layering of frame upon frame in pursuit of the elusive understanding of desire. In the *Charmides*, it leads to a remarkable manipulation of the potential for revelation and concealment that a fictional first-person narration allows: insider dealing. Plato's flair for exploring and exploiting the possibilities of the dialogue form is unmatched. Socrates' irony, however, his defining characteristic, further complicates any simple or direct articulation of ideas. The ironic master's profession of ignorance grounds each dialogue's progression towards knowledge. The move towards the abstract, the definitional, the theoretical, the authoritative is constantly in dynamic tension with the cut and thrust of personal exchange with its sardonic doubts and sly persuasions. Plato's Socrates inextricably intertwines the ironic and iconic. Yet for all this dizzy brilliance of writing there is still a critical and polemical move towards claiming a special status for philosophy. Within the competing disciplinary and institutional claims to authoritative *logos*, philosophy aims to ring-fence its own privileged conception of what it means 'to give an account', 'to know something'. Philosophy arrogates to itself true knowledge and true teaching. That is its claim to authority. What remains especially engaging – fascinating, difficult, frustrating – about Plato is that this claim to authority is inextricably bound up with the image of the calmly ironic Socrates, prodding and challenging and annoying those he meets.

III

To turn from Plato's elegant, engaging conversation to Aristotle's treatises can be something of a shock. Aristotle's prose is austere, even stark, technical, and although it has its own power to engage the reader, it is not through dramatization, characterization or the charm or seduction of its imagery. This blanching out of Plato's various negotiations with the polis and its forms of social exchange is at one crucial level a fundamental element in a new construction of the style or image of the philosopher, and we will be looking at that shortly. But there is another aspect that needs to be considered first, namely, the unique production of Aristotle's corpus.

Aristotle (born 384 BCE) came from Stagira in northern Greece. He moved to Athens where he became a member of the circle around Plato in Plato's Academy, the institutional focus for Plato's philosophical project. He stayed and studied for twenty years, but left Athens when Plato died in 347 (the time when Olynthus had just fallen to Philip – the subject of Demosthenes' *Olynthiac* orations). Shortly after, he became tutor to Alexander, Philip's son. (The intimate connection between the greatest philosopher of the age and the greatest military leader of the age is a stirring prospect – but only novelists have been able to uncover any tangible outcome of such an educational and imperialistic partnership.) He returned to Athens in 335 where he set up his own school in the Lyceum. He left Athens again in 322 for Chalcis on the island of Euboea near Athens, where he died within the year.[43] There is every reason to assume that Aristotle wrote throughout his long career. Indeed, Aristotle produced a huge number of works (over 150 titles are listed in ancient catalogues, although only 30 survive), and he wrote on a huge range of subjects, from political philosophy, to biology, to logic, to poetics . . . There is an ancient story that Theophrastus inherited Aristotle's library when Aristotle died. (Theophrastus became head of the Lyceum when its founder died.) Theophrastus passed the library to Neleus his nephew, who took it to the city called Scepsis in Asia Minor, where

---

[43] Elegant accounts of Aristotle's life and work in Barnes ed. (1995), 1–26 and Lloyd (1968).

he hid it in a cave. Two centuries later the rotting manuscripts were rediscovered and taken to Athens and thence to Rome where one Andronicus, a philosopher of the Peripatetic school, prepared an edition, from which all modern editions are descended.

This anecdote, unlike so many biographical tales from the ancient world, is given some credence by scholars; but whatever the historical accuracy of the story, the edition of Andronicus does highlight the particular problem of Aristotle's writing. For Aristotle's syntax is as restricted and as spare as Plato's is intricate and sinuous; the argument is often hard to follow because of its abrupt transitions and its lack of summary or transitional paragraphs; there are few signs of the sort of careful writing over, that one associates with the published works of Plato, Isocrates, Lysias or Demosthenes. Ancient commentators suggest that some of Aristotle's writings were produced for a general public (exoteric), and some were aimed specifically at the members of his school (esoteric) – and modern scholars have argued that the texts of Aristotle are not merely 'esoteric' – texts for his pupils – but are actually made up of lecture notes – that is, summaries of arguments which need the explication of commentary to become the full expression of a thesis. Hence the lack of examples, the lack of any easy transitional or connective paragraphs, and the relentless austerity. What's more, the assumption that Aristotle continued to work over some of this material has been used to explain some of the repetitions and inconsistencies within his corpus (the sort of rough edges that would have been smoothed out, it is assumed, by the polishing of a more formal release of the work).

If Aristotle's extant writings are in large part at least lecture notes, edited or compiled by Andronicus, it certainly changes the manner in which they should be read and appreciated. The harshness of expression, the lack of transition, the density of articulation requires the expansion of a reader's explication and exploration. Perhaps all texts need such work from a reader. But Aristotle and the peculiarities of this textual production take to an extreme such a dynamic – and we must take special care when we try to trace his precise techniques of persuasiveness. Whatever the story we tell, however, about why Aristotle's prose has the form it has, it is the case that its austerity has had a profound effect on the history of science and philosophy in the West.

Now, where Plato's dialogues often seem to resist systematic and direct expression, Aristotle is passionate about formalism. It is particularly fascinating to see how Aristotle takes several of the subjects that dominate early writing – and that I have been discussing in this book

– and sets out to produce exhaustive and systematic descriptions.[44] Take the issue of causality, responsibility, reason – *aitia*. Herodotus set 'the cause' of the conflict between Persia and Greece as the thematic heading at the end of his first paragraph; similarly Thucydides offered 'the real cause' of the Peloponnesian war – Spartan concern for the rise of Athenian power – as his opening focus. In both cases, the historian goes on to explore causality in a variety of ways and with a variety of techniques. Aristotle, however, makes explicit a *theory* of causation: he constructs a model which aims to be exhaustive, systematic and analytical – the hugely influential concept of 'the four causes' [*aitiai*]. He introduces the 'four causes' in the *Physics*:

In one way the cause is said to be the existing thing out of which something comes to be, e.g. the bronze of the statue . . . Another is the form or model [*paradeigma*]: this is the *logos* of what-it-is-to-be, and its *genera* . . . Furthermore, that from which the primary origin of change and rest e.g. the responsible deliberation or father of the child, and in general the agent of the thing produced, and the changer of the thing changed. Moreover, there is the end [*telos*]. This is that for the sake of which e.g. health of walking: for why does he walk? In order, we say, to be healthy, and in so saying we think we have given the reason [*aitia*].[45]

This is a typical passage of Aristotle: dense, with a minimum of exemplification, lack of transition or connection between the four ideas. Aristotle is facing the question of why things are how they are. If we cannot answer the questions prompted by the Four Causes, he claims, we cannot properly and fully *know* the objects of which we speak. True knowledge – *epistêmê*, as Plato also had used the term – means being able to explain why things are the way they are, and for a full explanation the categories of description are (1) the material cause – that is, of what material is something formed e.g. the bronze of a statue; (2) the formal cause: what essence does something have – that is, what makes a statue a statue (rather than a house or a spear)? (3) the efficient cause: what agent produced the object and how? Who sculpted the sculpture? (4) the final cause: what is the aim, goal or end of an object? What is a statue produced *for*? These four categories of argument together provide a formal discourse of *aitiai* in which knowledge of the world is to be articulated.[46]

---

[44] For good introductions to Aristotle's thought and writing, see Lloyd (1968), Lear (1988) and Barnes ed. (1995) – which has a huge bibliography on many aspects of Aristotle's work, conveniently organized.   [45] Aristotle, *Physics* 2. 3, 194b23–35.
[46] Good introductory discussion in Hankinson (1995), with further bibliography 327 and 353–4. See also, for Artistotle's theory of how knowledge is produced, his *Posterior Analytics* and *Prior Analytics*, discussed briefly below.

Aristotle goes on to investigate the relationship between these four methods of explanation, and even introduces some further interstitial factors (like 'drugs', causal intermediaries, through which action may be brought to completion). What matters here, however, is the drive towards system – a formal model, which aims to define what can be known and how. This is a different *type* of argument from the sophistication of Thucydides or Herodotus: a difference which is not merely reducible to the obvious difference of genre between history and philosophy. Both genres are aiming at explanatory description: but where Thucydides and Herodotus revel in the suggestiveness of dramatic juxtaposition, the hidden play of motive in the performance of direct speech, and the engaged narrator's discerning judgement, Aristotle seeks to remove the narrator's voice and the lure of narrative, stating the case as a general principle, and striving to link statements by the explicit devices of exemplification, hypothesis and deduction. The authority of Aristotle stems from the control and exclusivity of empirical description supported by logical reasoning.

Aristotle's descriptions of the natural world go far beyond the descriptions we saw in, say, *Airs, Waters, Places*, which is, of course, at least two generations earlier, or the 'wonders' recorded by Herodotus. He collects a vast data base of material on animals, for example, not only in the *History of Animals*, but also in the *On the Parts of Animals, On the Generation of Animals, On the Movement of Animals*. In this Aristotle is fascinated by how the different parts of animals can be categorized to reveal relationships between them. It is in this area of Aristotle's scientific work that it has proved easiest to show how the principle of empirical description supported by logical reasoning is an ideal that is less transparent in practice.[47] Thus Aristotle's descriptions owe more to inherited views of the world than he might like to have us believe. When female sheep, goats and pigs are said definitively to have fewer teeth than the males of the species – something that modern science resolutely disagrees with – it is reasonable to see such observation as being dependent on Aristotle's ideological declaration that 'a woman is a defective man' rather than on the precisions of empirical testing or the logic of deductive reasoning.[48] Indeed, Man – an adult Greek male – all too often emerges as the king-pin of the descriptive system – the perfect end-point by which the development of the rest of the world can be evaluated.

[47] See Gotthelf and Lennox edd. (1985); and especially Lloyd (1983).
[48] Aristotle, *Historia Animalium* 501b19 – discussed by Lloyd (1983), 102–4.

In the field of rhetoric, as we have seen, Aristotle prides himself on having produced the most extensive and exhaustive account of this branch of learning. In it, he catalogues the types of rhetoric (epideictic, forensic, deliberative) and the types of argument (the enthymeme) and proofs (and we have seen how difficult it can be to utilize such distinctions rigorously). In the field of political theory, Aristotle produces both a theoretical treatise on the nature of interaction in the state (the *Politics*) and also a descriptive catalogue of 158 constitutions of city states (a work undertaken largely by his pupils). In each of these areas, we see a similar turn: the laying down of principle, the process of definition, followed by reasoned development, together with an aim of the exhaustive reviewing of the relevant evidence. In each of these cases, we see an area of thought which many had reflected on, becoming the object of formal and systematic study – subject to Aristotle's methodological procedures.

For all of this work, logical argument is the basis and benchmark. (Aristotle is often praised for his 'scientific' or 'mathematical' rigour.) Aristotle himself points out that when it came to logic as a discipline, 'it is not the case that part had been worked out in advance and part had not' – as with politics, rhetoric, natural history – 'instead, nothing existed at all'.[49] Aristotle claims that he himself is the first person to try to construct a systematic, theoretical understanding not just of argument in general but, more specifically, of 'correct inference'. It is within this field that what is meant by Aristotle's scientific rigour is most in evidence (and Aristotle's contribution to the history of logic is truly foundational and impossible to overestimate). Here is the first paragraph of the treatise *Prior Analytics*, a piece which lays out some of the groundwork for the *Posterior Analytics*, whose primary subject is the theory of demonstration – how knowledge is produced:

First is needed a declaration of the scope and nature of the enquiry – namely, demonstration and demonstrative knowledge. Then a definition of 'premiss', 'term', and 'syllogism', what is a perfect and what an imperfect syllogism. After this, what it is to be or not to be 'wholly contained' and what we mean by predicated of all or of none.[50]

The first verb here is an infinitive in Greek, without a subject ('First to say . . .', *'prôton eipein,* for which can be understood 'it is necessary . . .'), and the expression of topic (literally 'about what and of what', *peri ti kai*

[49] Aristotle, *Sophistical Refutations* 34, 183b34–6. Aristotle's Logic is finely introduced by Smith in Barnes ed. (1995), 27–65, with bibliography 308–23.
[50] Aristotle, *Prior Analytics* 1. 1, 24a10–16.

tinos) could not be more bare: 'demonstration [*apodeixis*] and demonstrative knowledge [*apodeiktikê epistêmê*]'. The word *apodeixis* is the same term as Herodotus' description of his project [*apodexis*, in its Ionic spelling], which I translated before as 'presentation', or 'display'. *Apodeixis* is the topic of discussion now, and a very different sort of performance is under way. What is at stake for Aristotle here is the relation between true knowledge [*epistêmê*] and the proces of demonstration as a logical process. *Apodeixis* is no longer the name of prose's captivating narrative performance, but the subject of an enquiry into a genre of argument where content is wholly subordinate to form: 'If M is predicated of all N and all O there can be no syllogism. The positive relation of terms is illustrated by the terms substance-animal-man; the negative relation by substance-animal-number (substance is the middle term)'.[51] The terms of this argument are so abstract and generalized that they can be replaced with letters, and those central categories of Greek enquiry, man and beast, existence and number, are tokens to explain a logic, rather than as objects of scrutiny in themselves. Here is the *telos* of the move to formal argument. The contrast between Herodotus and Aristotle could not be more marked.

Yet almost every word in the opening paragraph of the *Prior Analytics* has a non-technical sense. 'Syllogism' [*sullogismos*] could be translated as 'deduction', and in its regular usage implies 'reckoning'. 'Predicate' [*katêgoreisthai*] is a legal term for accusation and thus extremely common in litigious Athens. 'Perfect' [*teleion*] and 'imperfect' [*ateles*] are words used of sacrificial victims. Perhaps only *protasis*, 'premiss', is a term which could not be readily used in another less specialized field of language. The words may be familiar, but the expression is difficult by virtue of its technicality (simple though it would probably be to Aristotelian scholars, hardened by long study).

This remark about Aristotelian scholars is not merely facetious. Aristotle adopts and refines and redefines regular vocabulary into a technical and specific discourse which requires from the reader a commitment to a set of terms, procedures, and argumentation, if it is to be read and comprehended adequately. The word *legomen*, 'we mean', is the only verb with a subject in that opening paragraph of the *Prior Analytics*. It may seem the weakest form of self-announcement. It betokens nonetheless a collusion between reader and text. To enter the world of Aristotle's prose is to follow the dictates of its own

---

[51] Aristotle, *Prior Analytics* 1. 5, 27a18–22.

regulatory system of logical deduction and delimited expression (which is why it is so hard to dip into Aristotle's writing, as my rebarbatively obscure second quotation from the *Prior Analytics* should have demonstrated). Plato's Socrates made a point of speaking to anyone: Aristotle demands to speak to you only as philosopher to philosopher.

It is this power of a *logical system* that causes Aristotle to be so readily taken up by medieval theologians in the West (as well as by the Arabic empire and by medieval Jewish scholarship). All the prose I have been discussing so far in this book has made an issue of self-placement: where you come from, how you create an image of your self, how you present character, how you give yourself authority to speak. Aristotle's logic, the ground of all his writing, seems to offer a promise of an argument without a narrator, without self-presentation: Aristotle makes a hero of *logos* itself. Where the success and privilege of *logos* once depended on a persuasive performance for an audience in a context, argument now is to have a decontextualized, impersonal framing, and its own, internal rules of success. Aristotle – who becomes *the* authority figure of authority figures, of course – demands that authority exists in the relation between sentences, and not in the relation between speaker and audience. Aristotle's contribution to prose: abstract, formal argument is now *to speak for itself.*

IV

Aristotle is often praised for the scientific rigour of his argumentation. I want to end this chapter by taking a step back from Aristotle's attempt to make logical argument as close as possible to mathematics, to an earlier scientific regime, epitomized by the Hippocratic corpus. As we saw in the introduction, the Hippocratic corpus is collection of medical texts, passed down to us under the name of the doctor Hippocrates, although they are written over an extended period of time and cannot have been written by one man, let alone by the celebrated medical founder who gave his name to the 'Hippocratic Oath'. I am going to concentrate on a single text called *On the Diseases of Virgins*, which is roughly contemporary with Herodotus and *Airs, Waters, Places* (and thus offers a pleasing circle back to the beginning of the book). This treatise is also revelatory about Greek scientific prose in a way that Aristotle's treatises on logic cannot be.

On the Diseases of Virgins is barely two pages long and of uncertain origin.[52] It is, however, not only fascinating for what it tells us about scientific method; it also gives us precious insight into gender relations from a medical viewpoint at this period.[53] *On the Diseases of Virgins* begins with the briefest of methodological statements that to know the nature [*phusis*] of a disease properly – which is the job of the discipline [*technê*] to find out – the disease must be traced in each stage from its diagnosis. By now, it should be clear that the search for *phusis* and the appeal to *technê* indicate the writer's engagement in the most up-to-date theoretical debate. By this statement, he – and we may assume that the author of this treatise like all the writers discussed in this book, is a man – also is placing himself in the middle of the new medicine of the Ionian East. The writers of the Hippocratic corpus explicitly rejected explanations of disease that relied on divine causation, and, in particular, dismissed diagnostic or curative practices that depended on what they were keen to stigmatize as superstition, magic or religious fakery. Disease is physical and must be understood and treated as such through the doctor's skill. (That 'epilepsy' is called in standard Greek 'the holy disease' [*hiera nosos*] provokes particular polemic, especially against the practices of temples and priests in the treatment of illness.) Hence, towards the end of *On the Diseases of Virgins*, the doctor comments 'when a female recovers mentally, the women make holy offerings to Artemis, especially of their most expensive robes, which is what the soothsayers command – but the women are being lied to and deceived'.

How, then, does the doctor in this religious society construct an authoritative position from which to advise men and women on life and death matters? The fundamental claim of this treatise is to offer a comprehensive physical *aitia* for what might seem the most irrational and psychological of conditions – a young girl's emotional trauma, which turns into self-destructive behaviour: a disease known colloquially, he tells us, as 'the horrors', *phobera*. Let us look at the description of the condition first:

Virgins, when they reach the age of marriage, but do not have sex with a man, suffer this more, at the onset of their periods; before, they do not have particularly bad experiences with it. For after, blood gathers in the womb, to flow out. When the mouth of the womb is not yet opened, and blood flows all the more copiously because of diet and the growth of the body, then the blood which does not have a route out, rushes from the excess to the heart and the diaphragm. When they fill, the heart becomes sluggish. Then from the sluggishness, numbness.

[52] See King (1998), 76: she thinks it is probably late 5th/early 4th century BCE.
[53] Best discussion is King (1998), 75–98. Crucial background also in Dean-Jones (1994), Lloyd (1983), 58–111, and Rihll (1999).

The doctor explains that puberty, with the growth of the body and increase of consumption of food, produces more blood in the female body, as the onset of a girl's periods indicate. Unless the mouth of the womb is properly opened – which means by having sex with a man – the blood cannot get out, and rises up through the body to the heart, which becomes sluggish and results in 'numbness' [*narkê*]. The image of the female body is of a sort of jar with connecting tubes: the blood should flow out copiously; if not, it rises till the jar becomes full, and thus pressure results, pressure on the heart. A woman's blood-flow is the physical cause of the symptoms of this disease.

This theoretical model of the body and the role of the flow of blood in it is supported by the buttresses of common knowledge.[54] The passage is introduced by the statement that 'women suffer more than men [from mental diseases involving exaggerated terrors] because female nature is less robust and weaker' . This generalization of the relative strength of men and women is a commonplace of agreed knowledge. Similarly, *narkê*, 'numbness', is explained in the sentence immediately after this passage with a homely analogy: numbness is like when you sit still too long in one position and your feet and hands 'go to sleep' and tingle. This is from the restriction of blood flow, too. What is more, the description of the female body also utilizes the most evident of everyday observations: a sign of puberty is the growth of the body. The technical, scientific model of the body is thus anchored in the cultural expectation of uncontested knowledge.

The doctor goes on with increasingly technical vocabulary to develop his model of blood-flow through the veins, and in particular the danger of restricted flow. For with restricted flow, the collected blood can putrefy:

When this is the condition, the woman becomes mad from the inflammation [*oxu-phlegmasiê*], she becomes murderous from the putrefaction [*sêpêdôn*] and from the intensity she becomes afraid and fears; and from the pressure around the heart, she takes on a desire for hanging, from the evil quality of the blood, the frenzied and disturbed spirit draws evil on itself.

The physical condition of the female has a psychological impact (as is so often proposed for women in the Western tradition).[55] The inflammation of the blood causes mental instability, and the rotting blood makes her murderous, and the intensity – the heat of the inflammation –

---

[54] See King (1998), 75–98, and especially Lloyd (1983).
[55] King (1998); also e.g. Showalter (1985).

produces terror in her. In Greek literature and especially in Greek tragedy, women – those figures of the male imagination – all too often show the psychological disturbances of madness, terror or murderousness. Here each and all of those states of mind find a cause in the corrupted blood of the virgin who remains too long a virgin, and thus allows the flow of her blood to become blocked.

There is indeed a remarkable list of symptoms offered by the doctor:

This condition orders them to leap around, to fall into wells, and to hang themselves, as if that were a better course of action and had a remarkable benefit. When they are without such fantasies, there is a certain pleasure from which she desires death as if it were a good thing.

This is a fascinating description which mixes folk-lore, cultural ideals and medical observation in a combination which is hard to unravel. 'To leap around' implies a lack of control in a rather general way (which has often been applied to the mad and the adolescent). 'To fall into wells', however, is a precise action which is extremely hard for us to evaluate. Is this meant to be a typical sign of mad female behaviour, particularly at adolescence? It is not mentioned by anyone else, however, as a particular sign of female behaviour, mad or sane. Or is it meant to be an extreme or even outlandish example of the sort of irrational and self-destructive impulse any girl suffering from 'the horrors' might perform? Is it meant to recall the well as the place where women gather to talk while collecting water – suggesting a connection between the normality of female life and the reversal of such behaviour in madness? 'Hanging oneself', however, the third symptom, is more than just a case of self-destructive violence (which is still in modern Western culture associated particularly with adolescence). For hanging is also a form of suicide thought to be specifically appropriate for women in Greek cultural imagination, which also seems to have connected the act of self-strangulation with the idea of the restriction of blood-flow (unlike falling on a sword or other forms of bloody self-violence).[56] Hanging, that is, is not only a female type of self-slaughter, but may be thought to have a connection with the disease itself. A story of constriction . . .

The final symptom of girls without visions is 'to desire death'. Again, this is more than a point about female adolescent morbidity. For there is a standard motif of Greek culture that when a girl of marriagable age dies before her wedding, she is said to take Hades, the god of death, as a lover, or 'to marry Hades'. This can be seen on tombstones and is even

[56] See Loraux (1987); King (1983).

sung about on the tragic stage.[57] The doctor's recognition of a symptom draws on the discourse of ritual for its persuasiveness. The young woman desires death – as is known from the ceremonials all around.

This account of the disease, then, combines a theory-laden description of the female body and its tubes and blood flow, with homely images of everyday life, and with the ideological stereotypes of what a woman is. It aims to give a physical explanation of a disease, and its fundamental claim to authority is through material description and its testability. It offers the reader the power of understanding a woman's behaviour – both her action and her psychological state – through her body, whose internal workings are laid open to comprehension. It is not merely the power of description, however, that grounds the doctor's authority: it is also his ability to predict (and if not cure, at least anticipate and explain the failure to cure). Thus immediately after his description of the symptoms of these girls, he first castigates women who make offerings to Artemis when a cure does take place (in the lines I quoted earlier), and then offers his own summary and cure:

The release for this disease is when there is no longer a blockage to the flow of blood. I instruct virgins, whenever they experience such a condition, to have sex with a man as soon as possible. If they become pregnant, they become healthy. If not either at maturity or a little later, she will be overcome, if not by this, by another disease. Of the women who do get married, the sterile suffer from this more.

The summary sentence contrasts strikingly with the previous image of the women dedicating costly dresses to the goddess Artemis on the advice of soothsayers. Instead of such ritual thanksgiving, the doctor explains the physical basis of the change back to health. The blockage is cleared. The doctor's recommended cure, however, takes his medical theory back into the arena of social values. The virgin who has this disease should 'have sex with a man as soon as possible'. The term I have translated 'have sex with' is *xunoikein* – which implies also 'to set up house [*oikos*] together [*xun*]'. The cure cannot be merely physical but must also have a social framework. So the young woman who gets pregnant will be healthy: on the one hand, this is a logical extension of the doctor's definition of the malady. If the build-up of blood is the problem, the childbirth with its expulsion of blood, preceded by the cessation of periods, that is a drastically restricted production of blood, is a positive benefit. On the other hand, the requirement of pregnancy

[57] See Seaford (1987); Goldhill (1990b), 103–4.

chimes with the standard ideological expectation that a woman's role is precisely to marry and to bear her husband an heir. Hence, in the final lines, the double threat that, first, if a woman does not marry and have children, a disease will always get her (if not the specific condition of this treatise, then another . . .), and second that among married women [*êndrômenôn*: women who have been 'manned'], those who cannot have children will always have a higher incidence of such diseases. The doctor's cure is persuasive not only because it follows on from his physical theories, but also because it matches his audience's ideological beliefs. Science and social value march hand in hand.[58]

Scientific prose promotes the power of description as a way of comprehending the world, and in so doing appropriates and manipulates the ideology of its audience to help construct its own persuasiveness. It enables the reader to know what he sees – and thus constructs the authority of the writer. It produces a paradigm, a model for processing and comprehending the data of the world; science also produces the theory and the observations that can shift such paradigms. Greek medicine in the classical polis is a fundamental element of a shifting paradigm of the human body, and how it can be understood. This brief treatise, *On the Diseases of Virgins*, is testimony to the struggle of such a paradigm shift – a paradigm of which we are in all too many ways still the heirs.

This discussion of the development of the prose of philosophy and science has shown how contested and intricate an issue 'giving an account', *logon didonai*, becomes in the classical city. Plato's dialogues move towards a theoretical and delimited conception of what it means to use *logos* in such a way as to produce knowledge, *epistêmê*. Yet at the same time as Plato is developing the formal description of philosophy's argumentation and constructing philosophy as the authoritative model for understanding the world, he is also brilliantly adopting and adapting the persuasive, dramatic power of the dialogue format and its lures of narrative and characterization. Central to Plato's project is Socrates, the authority figure who claims and disclaims (his own) authority. Central to the paradoxical fascination of Plato is the strategic choice not to represent his own voice but always to remain concealed within and behind the conversation of the bare-footed wandering gadfly, questioning and teasing whomever he happens to meet. The move towards a

---

[58] On modern science and gender, see e.g. Keller (1985); Harraway (1991).

formal theory of argument, however, is fully instantiated in Aristotle's remarkable and innovative treatises on logic above all. Where each of Aristotle's works is committed to the systematic study of topics of enquiry developed in the previous generation, the basis of all his work is an argumentative rigour theorized in the treatises on logic. Here argument becomes its own master. Argument's truth or authority does not depend on an ability to persuade an audience, but on its own rules. The thrill and risk of the scene of debate become a different intellectual pleasure. The audience of democracy, a basic element of all the works I have been discussing, even in Plato's anti-democratic tirades, becomes silenced in Aristotle's logic. Science offers the ability to undertsand the world through its matrix of observation and theory; yet, as *On the Diseases of Virgins* showed, this scientific prose mixed cultural expectation, stereotypes, and polemical assertion with its technical theorizing on the body's blood flow. How the gendered body should be comprehended is the contested question of this work.

Where historical prose found authority in the critically evaluated narrative of events, where rhetoric found authority in persuasive performance, philosophy seeks to place authority in the power of argument itself, and the prose of medical science rests its authority on the power of description to make the world comprehensible. It is in the classical city that these disciplines are first developed and interact in what I have been calling a contest of voices. Each discipline commands a privileged place from which to speak to – and for – the citizen. It is this struggle over authority which makes prose the medium of the intellectual, cultural and social revolution of the Greek enlightenment.

V. CONCLUSION

There are two parts to this conclusion, first a look forward, and second a look backwards. The look forward is towards the continuing history of prose. The major genres – history, rhetoric, philosophy, science – which begin in the classical city, develop and become more clearly demarcated as generic traditions. There are more strongly articulated markers of belonging to a tradition – rules of the genre, as it were – and writers self-consciously affiliate themselves to such traditions and play with them. So, for example, if we were to move on fully five hundred years we would find that an orator like Aelius Aristides, writing in the second century CE in the Greek East, composes speeches which self-consciously echo the style, content and form of Isocrates (among his other performances). Or if we were to go to the second century BCE we could read Polybius' history of Rome's conquest of Greece which knowingly works within a tradition headed by Thucydides.

It is, however, the new genres of prose which especially merit attention here, and I would like to focus very briefly on five genres which have had a particular influence on Western culture. Together, they demonstrate the continuing interplay between cultural change and the history of prose, as each indicates a new way of articulating a relation with an audience and a new way of viewing the world.

The first is the novel. Although no ancient critic happens to name the novel as a genre, five complete texts and many fragments survive that show all the signs of a recognized and self-conscious form.[1] Each of the novels is a lengthy prose text with an erotic subject – usually involving the separation and final reunion of a young couple. The novels that are extant seem to have been written from the first century CE to the 4th century CE – during the Roman empire, that is – and are texts that seem to be for private reading. (The social context of the novel's production and consumption is unclear, though most modern critics agree at least that these are intellectually sophisticated works, written for a wide-ranging but educated audience, but without perhaps the status of the highest literature or the grandest forms of public performance.) Because the novels develop a particular view of what it means to experience

---

[1] The novels can most easily be read in translation in Reardon (1989). For introduction see e.g. Tatum ed. (1994); Morgan and Stoneman (1994); more fun in Konstan (1994); see also Goldhill (1995).

desire, and because their subject matter and private consumption seem to resist the public life of political power, they have been seen as evidence of a significant shift in the ideals of citizenship towards a new internalizing 'care for the self' – part of the milieu from which Christianity emerged. Greek novels are all too often forgotten in histories of the novel – but in the 16th and 17th centuries Heliodorus' *Aethiopica* and Longus' *Daphnis and Chloe* were especially influential.[2]

The novel reflects many traditions of prose: there are highly rhetorical speeches, dialogue with philosophical leanings, set piece descriptions of wonders, and historical accounts of battles, processions, and courts. One of the most obvious 'father figures' for the novel is Xenophon, the writer of the 4th century BCE, in his *Cyropaideia* (*The Education of Cyrus*) – a fictionalized history of the great king of the Medes, which has a celebrated erotic tale in it. Xenophon also writes Socratic dialogues (*Memorabilia*, *Oikonomos*), as I mentioned in the previous chapter, and histories both of Greece's wars, following on from Thucydides (the *Hellenica*), and of his own adventures as a mercenary fighting for a usurper to the Persian throne (the *Anabasis*), as well as political pamphlets and a manual on hunting. Xenophon is a remarkable figure, whose multiform output is unparalleled in the classical city: this extraordinary variety of writing (and adventurous life) demonstrates the productive vitality of the invention of prose – and, most importantly for my argument here, how such variety feeds into a continuing tradition in different ways.

The second genre is the letter.[3] Now letters, of course, have existed from the time that writing has existed. They certainly play a role in the classical city and its literature, and it is certainly not inconceivable that some of the letter-writing passed down to us in the name of Plato, say, may be genuine. But from the early Hellenistic period onwards, collections of letters circulate, written as if by a famous person of the past; so too do letters from a particular class of person ('letters of courtesans', 'letters of farmers'); there is even a novel in letters.[4] Letters offer the promise of a true picture of a writer's inner life – which is why they are so often the medium of forgery. Like the novel, they indicate a growing concern with the self, its revelation and control. While Lucian's 'Letters of Prostitutes' may offer a mildly pornographic (literally!) glimpse into what the whore is really like – a male fantasy, if ever

---

[2] See Doody (1998).
[3] On the letter, see Rosenmeyer (2001).
[4] Chion of Heraclea, as discussed by Rosenmeyer (2001), 234–52.

there was one – the letters of Paul of Tarsus show the potential power of such personal communications when they are aimed at a public.

The third genre is 'the life' – associated particularly with Plutarch, whose *Lives* remained one of the most read and most influential of all ancient texts until quite recently.[5] Biography makes exemplars of the great men of the past, and not only gives a moral and political understanding of an individual's history, but also constructs the heroic paradigms by which modern readers can strive to live their own lives. It makes the classical past 'classical' – a world populated by great men and great deeds which project the examples by which the present can be judged. It is not by chance that Plutarch lived near Delphi, the oracle at the centre of Greek religious life, in the first century CE, when Rome dominated the Mediterranean. Plutarch's work looks back to the great days of Greece as part of his negotiation of how Greeks are to live their lives now in this new world order. As with the letter, it is easy to trace crucial precursors in the writing I have been discussing in this book. The tradition of telling Socrates' life begins with Plato and Xenophon; Xenophon's *Agesilaus* records the great deeds of a Spartan hero. Writing biography draws on the past of Greek prose to find a fresh accommodation with the intellectual and political problems of the Empire in particular – and culminates in the revolutionary biographies of Jesus of Nazareth, and the hagiographic saints' lives of subsequent centuries.

The fourth genre, however, looks back more to Gorgias and his paradoxical and witty epideictic essays. This is the satirical essay/speech, which holds up a different mirror to the present, in order to mock contemporary failure to live up to its – to any – ideals. The leading writer here is Lucian, who came from Syria, and wrote in the second century CE. He is a central figure in the so-called 'Second Sophistic', the revival of Greek literary culture in the Empire, where there developed an Empire-wide institution of set-piece lecturing of all types, through which many a superstar performer made his name and fortune. Lucian's essays were particularly beloved of the humanists of the Renaissance. The Renaissance's turning back to the glories of Greece made heroes of Lucian and Plutarch who in their different ways were also obsessed with the relation between the present and the classical past. Again, the development of prose genres out of past models leads to a new and significant social and cultural form.[6]

---

[5] On Plutarch, see Duff (1999); and on his shift in reputation, Goldhill (2002).
[6] See Branham (1989); Robinson (1979).

The fifth genre that needs mentioning here is the Gospel.[7] The development of Christianity is, of course, one of the most far-reaching intellectual and political changes in the Roman Empire. The spread of Christianity – however it is explained – relied at least in part on the use of the texts of the Gospels and their persuasiveness. These are brief prose works in Greek which put together elements of wisdom literature (the circulation of a wise man's sayings), biography, miracle stories, fable, philosophy (especially in the case of John) and even the novel – into a surprising mélange that is difficult to pigeonhole. Religious commitment to a book (an idea which came from Judaism) is rare in Greco-Roman culture, which had no bible (although some minor sects such as Orphism did have its sacred volumes). Here again the circulation and absorption of a new prose genre is absolutely fundamental to a cultural revolution.

A history of prose, then, would take us far from democracy and the classical city. But these developments of different genres and new instantiations of old genres would also reveal prose's continuing and significant role in the changing culture of Greco-Roman society. A society's prose is a fundamental part of its critical imagination – how the world can be described and understood. Its generic innovations are integral to the major shifts in such critical imagination.

My final look backwards is not to summarize the argument of the previous chapters, but to draw out some connections and conclusions – and I have five brief points I want to make.

First, each of the prose authors I have looked at is concerned with developing a particular critical, evaluative viewpoint, and is aimed at constructing an authoritative voice for the writer. This is both sign and symptom of the competition around authority in the political and intellectual arenas of the classical city, and especially of the democratic city of Athens, the centre for such critical activity in the Greek-speaking world. The construction of authority takes different forms, from the self-presentation of the orator as a good citizen to the rigorous rules of pure logic. In each case, however, the audience of citizens that democracy creates is a crucial frame – even when, as in the case of Aristotle's logic, the force of his method depends on the silencing of such an audience in the name of the formal rules of argumentation. The invention of prose thus stages a contest over who has the privileged right to speak to and for the citizens.

---

[7] For the Gospel as genre see Burridge (1992).

Second – and this follows directly from the first – each of these prose texts demonstrates a self-conscious awareness of its own working. Writing history not only requires that the historian show an awareness of his methodology but also encourages such critical reading in its audiences. Rhetoric makes both performers and audience aware of the tricks of presentation – and thus demands a continuous manipulativeness, a game of bluff and counterbluff in the seductions of a persuasive performance. Socrates took as a motto that the unexamined life is not worth living, and Plato's focus on how arguments work, coupled with his own extraordinary narrative panache, enacts such a principle of self-scrutiny. The invention of prose brings a heightened, critical self-awareness of how language works.

Third, each of the genres I have been discussing reveals a particular concern with the idea of causality, responsibility, explanation – or, to put it in Greek, *aitia*. From Herodotus' version of why Greeks and Persians went to war, to Aristotle's systematic model of the 'four *aitiai*', to the doctor's explanation of why a disease has its peculiar symptoms, immense intellectual energy is spent in uncovering not just the explanatory connections between events – why x led to y – but also the abstract principles which are inherent in events or phenomena ('nature', 'reason', 'the human' and so forth). Such explanations empower the reader to understand the world – and to see reality's structure and not just phenomena. That's the knowledge promised by the search for an *aitia*. What is more, in all the works I have been discussing there is a turn away from the divine as a form of explanation or motivation, and a focus on man as a responsible and instrumental actor. It would be too simple to make a stark contrast between Homer's world (where gods so often make things happen) and the (democratic) city (where a man is responsible in law and in politics for his actions). None the less, Protagoras' slogan 'man is the measure of all things' would be unthinkable in the discourse of archaic society. The so-called intellectual enlightenment of the classical *polis* changes the way man sees himself in the world. With the invention of prose comes a new sense of man as a responsible and knowing agent.

Fourth, the different prose works construct different contracts with their readers – different expectations, different ideals of response. The variety is clear enough: Thucydides tells his readers he expects hard work, intellectual rigour and a commitment to the complexity of true understanding of complex events. Gorgias playfully tells his reader that he has been joking. Demosthenes tries to pull and push the audience into a collective opinion – with himself as leader of it. One thread that links the different relationships between author and audience, reader and text, is the question of the activity and passivity of the listener/reader. Thucydides' Cleon gives a political edge to such an idea: the citizen in the Assembly should be an active participant in the political process, not a passive spectator like an audience of a sophist's show. Gorgias makes an intellectual point of it, by theorizing the complete passivity of anyone listening to his *logos*. Plato's dialogues constantly cajole and encourage and tease the reader into doing philosophy – participating in life-changing study and not just reading. The invention of prose makes the reader or audience a character and a question at the scene of performance.

My final point is best phrased as a question. The invention of prose takes place at around the same time and place as the flowering of the new political system of democracy. The basis of democracy – the responsible citizen, the evaluating and participatory audience of citizens, openness of debate, the value of public decision-making, the primacy of the institutions of law and of the Assembly – have all found strong echoes in my description of the new genres of prose in the classical city. The question thus arises: is there any necessary connection between democracy and its forms of prose? I find it hard to see any direct, causal connections – and prose certainly exists outside democracy in the fifth and fourth centuries, and continues long after democracy (as we have seen). But I also find it hard to think of the invention of prose and the invention of democracy as unrelated developments. Democracy and the invention of prose proceed hand in hand. Indeed, it is not easy to imagine how a citizen could conceive of himself as a citizen without the performance of the law court and Assembly, without his sense of his city's history of war, without his awareness of Athens as a capital of culture. So perhaps it would be appropriate to conclude at least that the invention of prose helped produce the democratic subject.

The invention of prose, then, is the invention of the medium in which the intellectual and political revolutions of the classical city were performed. I hope this survey will have indicated something of the ferment of that cultural moment, and some of the implications of such a moment, which are still being felt and worked through in Western society. For the invention of prose raises fundamental questions about the relation between man, knowledge and authority in society – and how the language we use of the world matters.

BIBLIOGRAPHY: WORKS CITED

Alcock, S. and Osborne, R. edd. (1994): *Placing the Gods. Sanctuaries and Sacred Space in Ancient Greece* (Oxford).

Andrewes, A. (1956): *The Greek Tyrants* (London).

Annas, J. (1981): *An Introduction to Plato's Republic* (Oxford).

Arthur, M. (1982): 'Cultural Strategies in Hesiod's *Theogony*: Law, Family and Society', *Arethusa* 15, 63–82.

—— (1983): 'The Dream of a World without Women: Poetics and Circles of Order in the *Theogony* Prooemium', *Arethusa* 16, 97–116.

Barnes, J. (1979): *The Presocratic Philosophers* (London).

—— ed. (1995): *The Cambridge Companion to Aristotle* (Cambridge).

Bernal, M. (1987): *Black Athena* (London).

Boedeker, D. (1987): 'The Two Faces of Demaratus', *Arethusa* 20, 184–201.

—— (1988): 'Protesilaus and the End of Herodotus' *Histories*', *CA* 7, 30–48.

Boegehold, A. and Scafuro, A. edd. (1994): *Athenian Identity and Civic Ideology* (Baltimore and London).

Bourdieu, P. (1977): *Outline of a Theory of Practice*, trans R. Nice (Cambridge).

Branham, B. (1989): *Unruly Eloquence: Lucian and the Comedy of Traditions* (Cambridge, Mass.).

Brickhouse, T. and Smith, N. (1989): *Socrates on Trial* (Oxford).

Burnyeat, M. (1976): 'Protagoras and Self-Refutation in later Greek Philosophy', *The Philosophical Review* 85, 44–69.

—— (1990): *The Theaetetus of Plato* (Indianapolis).

—— (1994): 'Enthymeme: Aristotle on the Logic of Persuasion', in Furley and Nehamas edd. (1994).

—— (1996): 'Enthymeme: Aristotle on the Rationality of Rhetoric', in Rorty ed. (1996).

Burridge, R. (1992): *What are the Gospels? A Comparison with Greco-Roman Biography* (Cambridge).

Buxton, R. (1982): *Persuasion in Greek Culture* (Cambridge).

Calame, C. (1997): *Choruses of Young Women in Ancient Greece*, 2nd edition (Lanham and London).

Cameron, A. and Kuhrt, A. edd, (1983): *Images of Women in Antiquity* (London and Melbourne).

Carawan, E. (1998): *Rhetoric and the Law of Draco* (Oxford).

Carey, C. ed. (1989): *Lysias: Selected Speeches* (Cambridge).

—— (1992): *Greek Orators VI: Apollodorus Against Neaira [Demosthenes 59]* (Warminster).

Cartledge, P. (1979): *Sparta and Lakonia: a Regional History* (London).

—— (1993): *The Greeks: A Portrait of Self and Other* (London).

Cartledge, P, Millett, P. and Todd, S. edd. (1990): *Nomos* (Cambridge).

Castriota, D. (1992): *Myth, Ethos and Actuality: Official Art in fifth-century B.C, Athens* (Madison).

Clarke, H. (1981): *Homer's Readers* (Newark).

Classen, W. ed. (1976): *Sophistik* (Darmstadt).

Clay, J. (1989): *The Politics of Olympus* (Princeton).

Cogan, M. (1981): *The Human Thing: The Speeches and Principles Of Thucydides' Histories* (Chicago).

Cohen, D. (1991): *Law, Sexuality and Society* (Cambridge).

Cole, T. (1991): *The Origins of Rhetoric in Ancient Greece* (Baltimore).

Connor, W. R. (1971): *The New Politicians of Fifth-Century Athens* (Princeton).

—— (1984): *Thucydides* (Princeton).

—— (1987): 'Tribes, Festivals and Processions: Civic Ceremonial and Political Manipulation in Archaic Greece', *JHS* 107, 40–50.

Coventry, L. (1990): 'The Role of the Interlocutor in Plato's Dialogues: Theory and Practice', in Pelling ed. (1990).

Crane, G. (1996): *The Blinded Eye: Thucydides and the New Written Word* (London).

Davidson, J. (1997): *Courtesans and Fishcakes* (London).

Davies, J. (1993): *Democracy and Classical Greece*, 2nd ed (London).

Day, J. (1994): *Plato's Meno in Focus* (London).

Dean-Jones, L. (1994): *Women's Bodies in Classical Greek Science* (Oxford).

de Polignac, F. (1995): *Cults, Territory and the Origins of the Greek City State* (Chicago).

Derrida, J. (1981): *Dissemination*, trans. B. Johnson (Chicago).

Detienne, M. (1986): *The Creation of Mythology* (Chicago).

Dewald, C. (1987): 'Narrative Surface and Authorial Voice in Herodotus' *Histories*', *Arethusa* 20, 147–70.

—— (1997): 'Wanton Boys, Pickled Heroes, and Gnomic Founding Fathers: Strategies of Meaning at the End of Herodotus' *Histories*', in Roberts, Dunn, and Fowler edd. (1997).

Doody, M. (1998): *The True History of the Novel* (London).

Dougherty, C and Kurke, L. edd (1993): *Cultural Poetics in Archaic Greece* (Cambridge).

Dover, K. (1968): *Lysias and the Corpus Lysiacum* (Berkeley).

—— (1978): *Greek Homosexuality* (Cambridge, Mass.).

Duff, T. (1999): *Plutarch's Lives: Exploring Virtue and Vice* (Oxford).

Easterling, P. ed. (1997): *The Cambridge Companion to Greek Tragedy* (Cambridge).

Edwards, M. and Usher, S. edd. (1985): *Greek Orators 1: Antiphon and Lysias* (Warminster).

Euben, J. P. (1997): *Corrupting Youth: Political Education, Democratic Culture and Political Theory* (Princeton).

Falkner, T., Felson, N. and Konstan, D. edd. (1999): *Contextualizing Classics: Ideology, Performance, Dialogue* (Lanham).

Farrar, C. (1988): *The Origins of Democratic Thinking* (Cambridge).

Fehling, D. (1989): *Herodotus and his 'Sources'*, trans. J. Howie (Leeds).

Ferrari, G. (1987) *Listening to the Cicadas: a Study of Plato's* Phaedrus (Cambridge).

Figueira, T. and Nagy, G. edd. (1985): *Theognis of Megara* (Baltimore).

Fine, G. (1992): 'Inquiry in the *Meno*', in Kraut ed. (1992).

Finley, J. (1967): *Three Essays on Thucydides* (Cambridge, Mass.).

Finley, M. (1981): *Economy and Society of Ancient Greece* (London).

—— (1983): *Politics in the Ancient World* (Cambridge).

Fisher, N. (2001): *Aeschines: Against Timarchos* (Oxford).

Foley, H. (1994): *The Homeric Hymn to Demeter* (Princeton).

Ford, A. (1999): 'Reading Homer from the Rostrum: Poems and Laws in Aeschines' *Against Timarchus*', in Goldhill and Osborne edd. (1999).

—— (forthcoming): *The Invention of Poetry* (Princeton).

Fornara, C. (1971): *Herodotus: an Interpretative Essay* (Oxford).

Forrest, G. (1966): *The Emergence of Greek Democracy* (London).

Foucault, M. (1987): *The Use of Pleasure*, trans. R. Hurley (London).

Fowler, R. (1996): 'Herodotus and his Contemporaries', *JHS* 116, 62–87.

Foxhall, L. and Lewis, D. edd. (1996): *Greek Law in its Political Setting* (Oxford).

Furley, D. and Nehamas, A. edd. (1994): *Aristotle's Rhetoric*: Philosophical Essays (Princeton).

Gagarin, M. (1977): 'Socrates' *Hubris* and Alcibiades' Failures', *Phoenix* 31, 22–37.

—— (1986): *Early Greek Law* (Berkeley).

Gill, C. (1995) *Greek Thought* (Oxford).

Gill, C. and Wiseman, T. P. edd. (1993): *Lies and Fiction in the Ancient World* (Exeter).

Goldhill, S. (1986): *Reading Greek Tragedy* (Cambridge).

—— (1990): 'The Great Dionysia and Civic Ideology', in Winkler and Zeitlin edd. (1990).

—— (1990b): 'Character and Action, Representation and Reading', in Pelling ed. (1990).

—— (1991): *The Poet's Voice: Essays on Poetics and Greek Literature* (Cambridge).

—— (1995): *Foucault's Virginity: Ancient Erotic Fiction and the History of Sexuality* (Cambridge).

—— (1999): 'Body/Politics: Is there a History of Reading?', in Falkner, Felson and Konstan edd. (1999).

—— (2000): 'Civic Ideology and the Problem of Difference: The Politics of Aeschylean Tragedy, Once Again', *JHS* 120, 34–56.

Goldhill, S. (2002): *Who Needs Greek? Contests in the cultural History of Hellenism* (Cambridge).

Goldhill, S. and Osborne, R. edd. (1999): *Performance Culture and Democratic Athens* (Cambridge).

Gonzalez, F. (1998): *Dialectic and Dialogue* (Evanston).

Gordon, R. ed. (1981): *Myth, Religion and Society* (Cambridge).

Gotthelf, A. and Lennox, J. edd. (1985): *Philosophical Issues in Aristotle's Biology* (Cambridge).

Gould, J. (1983): 'Homeric Epic and the Tragic Moment' in *Aspects of Epic*, ed. Winnifrith, T., Murray, P., and Gransden, K. (London).

—— (1989): *Herodotus* (London).

Gould, T. (1990): *The Ancient Quarrel Between Poetry and Philosophy* (Princeton).

Gouldner, A. (1965): *Enter Plato* (London and New York).

Griswold, C. ed. (1988): *Platonic Writings, Platonic Readings* (London).

Guthrie, W. (1962–81): *A History of Greek Philosophy*, 6 vols (Cambridge).

Hall, E. (1989): *Inventing the Barbarian* (Oxford).

—— (1995): 'Law Court Dramas: the Power of Performance in Greek Forensic Oratory', *BICS* 40, 39–58.

—— (1996): *Aeschylus: Persians* (Warminster).

Halperin, D. (1990): *One Hundred Years of Homosexuality* (London and New York).

—— (1992): 'Plato and the Erotics of Narrativity', in R. Hexter and D. Selden edd. (1992).

Hankinson, J. (1995): 'Philosophy of Science' in Barnes ed. (1995).

Harraway, D. (1991): *Simians, Cyborgs and Women* (New York).

Harrison, T. (2000): *Divinity and History: The Religion of Herodotus* (Oxford).

Hartog, F. (1988): *The Mirror of Herodotus*, trans. J. Lloyd (Berkeley).

Heinimann, F. (1945): *Nomos und Phusis: Herkunft und Bedeutung einer Anithese im griechischen denken des 5 Jahrhunderts* (Basel).

Henderson, J. (2000): 'The Life and Soul of the Party: Plato's *Symposium*', in A. Sharrock and H. Morales edd. (2000).

Herington, J. (1991): 'The Closure of Herodotus' *Histories*', *ICS* 6, 149–60.

Hesk, J. (2000): *Deception and Democracy in Classical Athens* (Cambridge).

Hexter, R. and Selden, D. edd. (1992): *Innovations of Antiquity* (New York and London).

Hornblower, S. (1987): *Thucydides* (London).

—— (1991): *The Greek World 479–323 BC* (London).

—— (1991b): *A Commentary on Thucydides* Vol 1. (Oxford).

Humphreys, S. (1987): 'Law, Custom and Nature in Herodotus', *Arethusa* 20, 211–20.

Hunter, V. (1982): *Past and Process in Herodotus and Thucydides* (Princeton).

Immerwahr, H. (1966): *Form and Thought in Herodotus* (Cleveland).

Jarratt, S. (1991): *Rereading the Sophists: Classical Rhetoric Refigured* (Carbondale and Edwardsville).

Kahn, C. (1983): 'Drama and Dialectic in Plato's *Gorgias*', *Oxford Studies in Ancient Philosophy* 1, 75–121.

—— (1996): *Plato and the Socratic Dialogue: the Philosophical Use of a Literary Form* (Cambridge).

Keller, E. F. (1985): *Reflections on Gender and Science* (New Haven).

Kennedy, G. (1963): *The Art of Persuasion in Greece* (Princeton).

Kerferd, G. (1981): *The Sophistic Movement* (Cambridge).

King, H. (1983): 'Bound to Bleed: Artemis and Greek Women', in Cameron and Kuhrt edd. (1983).

—— (1998): *Hippocrates' Woman: Reading the Female Body in Ancient Greece* (London).

Kirk, G., Raven, J. and Schofield, M. (1983): *The Presocratic Philosophers* (Cambridge).

Konstan, D. (1994): *Sexual Symmetry: Love in the Ancient Novel and Related Genres* (Princeton).

Kraut, R. (1984): *Socrates and the State* (Princeton).

—— ed. (1992): *The Cambridge Companion to Plato* (Cambridge).

Lamberton, R. (1988): *Hesiod* (New Haven).

Lang, M. (1984): *Herodotean Narrative and Discourse* (Cambridge, Mass.).

Lateiner, D. (1977): 'No Laughing Matter: a Literary Tactic in Herodotus', *TAPA* 107, 173–82.

—— (1989): *The Historical Method of Herodotus* (Toronto).

Lear, J. (1988): *Aristotle: the Desire to Understand* (Cambridge).

Lloyd, A. (1990): 'Herodotus on Egyptians and Libyans', in *Entretiens Hardt* 35, 215–44 (Vandoeuvres-Genève).

Lloyd, G. (1968): *Aristotle* (Cambridge).

—— (1979): *Magic, Reason and Experience* (Cambridge).

—— (1983): *Science, Folklore and Ideology* (Cambridge).

—— (1987): *The Revolutions of Wisdom* (Berkeley).

Loraux, N. (1986): *The Invention of Athens*, trans. A. Sheridan (Cambridge, Mass.).

—— (1987): *Tragic Ways of Killing a Woman*, trans. A. Forster (Cambridge, Mass.).

—— (1993): *The Children of Athena* (Princeton).

McKim, R. (1985): 'Socratic Self-knowledge and "Knowledge of Knowledge" in Plato's *Charmides*', *TAPA* 115, 59–77.

MacDowell, D. (1982): *Gorgias: Encomium of Helen* (Bristol).

Mackie, H. (1996): *Talking Trojan* (Lanham).

Macleod, C. (1983): *Collected Essays* (Oxford).

Marincola, J. (2001): *Greek Historians* (Oxford).

Martin, R. (1984): 'Hesiod, Odysseus, and the Instruction of Princes', *TAPA* 114, 29–48.

—— (1989): *The Language of Heroes* (Ithaca).

Meier, C. (1990): *The Greek Discovery of Politics* (Cambridge, Mass.).

Miller, M. (1997): *Athens and Persia in the Fifth Century B.C.* (Cambridge).

Moles, J. (1993): 'Truth and Untruth in Herodotus and Thucydides', in Gill and Wiseman edd. (1993).

—— (1996): 'Herodotus warns the Athenians', *Papers of the Leeds Latin Seminar* 9, 259–84.

Monoson, S. (2000): *Plato's Democratic Entanglements: Athenian Politics and the Practice of Philosophy* (Princeton).

Morgan, J. and Stoneman, R. edd. (1994): *Greek Fiction: the Greek Novel in Context* (London).

Morris, I. (1987): *Burial and Ancient Society. The Rise of the Greek City State* (Cambridge).

Mueller, I. (1992): 'Mathematical Method and Philosophical Truth', in Kraut ed. (1992).

Murray, O. ed. (1990): *Sympotica* (Oxford).

Nagy, G. (1979): *The Best of the Achaeans* (Baltimore and London).

—— (1987): 'Herodotus the *logios*', *Arethusa* 20, 175–84.

—— (1990): *Pindar's Homer* (Baltimore).

Nehemas, A. (1998): *The Art of Living: Socratic Reflections from Plato to Foucault* (Berkeley).

—— (1999): *Virtues of Authenticity* (Princeton).

Neils, J. ed. (1992): *Goddess and Polis: the Panathenaic Festival in Ancient Athens* (Princeton).

Nightingale, A. (1995): *Genres in Dialogue* (Cambridge).

Nussbaum, M. (1986): *The Fragility of Goodness* (Cambridge).

Ober, J. (1989): *Mass and Elite in Democratic Athens: Rhetoric, Ideology and the Power of the People* (Princeton).

—— (1994): 'Civic Ideology and Counterhegemonic Discourse: Thucydides on the Sicilian Debate', in Boegehold and Scafuro edd. (1994).

—— (1998): *Political Dissent in Democratic Athens: Intellectual Critics of Popular Rule* (Princeton).

Omitowoju, R. (2002): *Rape and the Politics of Consent* (Cambridge).

Orwin, C. (1994): *The Humanity of Thucydides* (Princeton).

Osborne, R. (1985): 'Law in Action in Classical Athens' *JHS* 105, 40–58.

—— (1987): 'The Viewing and Obscuring of the Parthenon Frieze', *JHS* 107, 98–105.

—— (1993): 'Competitive Festivals and the Polis: a Context for Dramatic Festivals in Athens', in Sommerstein, Halliwell, Henderson and Zimmermann edd. (1993).

—— (1996): *Greece in the Making 1200–479 BC* (London).

—— (1998): *Archaic and Classical Greek Art* (Oxford).

—— ed. (2000): *Classical Greece* (Oxford).

Ostwald, M. (1986): *From Popular Sovereignty to the Rule of Law* (Berkeley).

Pelliccia, H. (1992): 'Sappho 16, Gorgias' *Helen*, and the Preface to Herodotus' *Histories*', YCS 29, 63–84.

Pelling, C. ed. (1990): *Characterization and Individuality in Greek Literature* (Oxford).

Pembroke, S. (1967): 'Women in Charge: the Function of Alternatives in Early Greek Tradition and the Ancient Idea of Matriarchy', *Journal of the Warburg and Courtauld Institutes* 30, 1–35.

Penwill, J. (1978): 'Men in Love: Aspects of Plato's *Symposium*', *Ramus* 7, 143–75.

Pollitt, J. (1972): *Art and Experience in Classical Greece* (Cambridge).

Poulakos, J. (1995): *Sophistical Rhetoric in Classical Greece* (Columbia, South Carolina).

Poulakos, T. ed. (1993): *Rethinking the History of Rhetoric* (Boulder).

Press, G. ed. (1993): *Plato's Dialogues: New Studies and Interpretation* (Lanham).

—— (2000): *Who Speaks for Plato? Studies in Platonic Anonymity* (Lanham).

Price, A. (1989): *Love and Friendship in Plato and Aristotle* (Oxford).

Price, J. (2001): *Thucydides and Internal War* (Cambridge).

Prier, R. (1989): *Thauma Idesthai: the Phenomenology of Sight and Appearance in Archaic Greece* (Tallahassee).

Raaflaub, K. (1987): 'Herodotus, Political Thought and the Meaning of History', *Arethusa* 20, 221–48.

Rawlings, H. (1975): *A Semantic Study of Prophasis to 400 B.C.*, *Hermes* Einzelschriften, 33.

Reardon, B. (1989): *Collected Ancient Greek Novels* (Berkeley).

Redfield, J. (1975): *Nature and Culture in the Iliad* (Chicago).

—— (1985): 'Herodotus the Tourist', *CP* 80, 97–118.

Rhodes, R. (1995): *Architecture and Meaning on the Athenian Acropolis* (Cambridge).

Rihll, T. (1999): *Greek Science* (Oxford).

Roberts, D., Dunn, F. and Fowler, D. edd. (1997): *Classical Closure: Reading the End in Greek And Latin Literature* (Princeton).

Robinson, C. (1979): *Lucian* (London).

Robinson, R. (1953): *Plato's Earlier Dialectic* (Oxford).

Robinson, T. (1979): *Contrasting Arguments: an edition of the Dissoi Logoi* (New York).

Romilly, J. de (1963): *Thucydides and Athenian Imperialism*, trans. P. Tody (Oxford).

—— (1992): *The Great Sophists in Periclean Athens*, trans. J. Lloyd (Oxford).

Romm, J. (1998): *Herodotus* (New Haven).

Rorty, A. ed (1996): *Essays in Aristotle's Rhetoric* (Berkeley).

Rose. P. (1992): *Sons of the Gods, Children of Earth* (Ithaca).

Rosenmeyer, T. (1955): 'Gorgias, Aeschylus and ἀπάτη', *AJP* 76, 225–60.

Rosenmeyer, P. (2001): *Ancient Epistolary Fictions* (Cambridge).

Rundle, D. (1998): '"Not so much Praise as Precept": Erasmus, Panegyric and the Renaissance Art of Teaching Princes', in Too and Livingstone edd. (1998).

Rusten, J. (1989): *Thucydides: the Peloponnesian War, Book II* (Cambridge).

Rood, T. (1998): *Thucydides: Narrative and Explanation* (Oxford).

Said, E. (1978): *Orientalism* (London).

Ste. Croix, G. de (1972): *The Origins of the Peloponnesian War* (London).

Saxenhouse, A. (1992): *Fear of Diversity: The Birth of Political Science in Ancient Greek Thought* (Chicago).

Sayre, K. (1995): *Plato's Literary Garden. How to Read a Platonic Dialogue* (Notre Dame).

Schiappa, E. (1990): 'Did Plato coin *Rhêtorikê*?', *AJP* 111, 457–70.

—— (1991): *Protagoras and Logos* (Columbia).

—— (1999): *The Beginnings of Rhetorical Theory in Classical Greece* (New Haven).

Schmid, T. (1998): *Plato's Charmides and the Socratic Ideal of Rationality* (Albany).

Scott, D. (1995): *Recollection and Experience: Plato's Theory of Learning and Its Successors* (Cambridge).

Seaford, R. (1987): 'The Tragic Wedding', *JHS* 107, 106–30.

Sealey, R. (1993): *Demosthenes and His Time* (Oxford).

Sebeok, T. and Brady, E. (1979): 'The Two Sons of Croesus: A Myth about Communication in Herodotus', *QUCC* 1, 7–22.

Segal, C. (1962): 'Gorgias and the Psychology of the Logos', *HSCP* 66, 99–155.

—— (1971): 'Croesus on the Pyre: Herodotus and Bacchylides', *WS* 5, 39–51.

Sharrock, A. and Morales, H. edd. (2000) *Intratextuality: Greek and Roman Textual Relations* (Oxford).

Showalter, E. (1985): *The Female Malady: Women, Madness and English Culture, 1830–1980* (New York).

Sinclair, R. (1988): *Democracy and Participation in Athens* (Cambridge).

Sinclair, T. (1976): 'Protagoras and Others. Socrates and his Opponents', in Classen ed. (1976).

Snodgrass, A. (1971): *The Dark Age of Greece* (Edinburgh).

—— (1980): *Archaic Greece* (Berkeley).

Sommerstein, A., Halliwell, S., Henderson, J., and Zimmermann, B. edd. (1993): *Tragedy, Comedy and the Polis* (Bari).

Stadter, P. ed. (1973): *The Speeches in Thucydides* (Chapel Hill).

Stahl, H-P. (1975): 'Learning Through Suffering', *YCS* 24, 1–36.

Stehle, E. (1997): *Performance and Gender in Ancient Greece* (Princeton).

Stewart, A. (1997): *Art, Desire and the Body in Ancient Greece* (Cambridge).

Stone, I.F. (1988): *The Trial of Socrates* (Boston).

Strauss, B. (1987): *Athens after the Peloponnesian War* (London and New York).

Swearingen, C. Jan (1991): *Rhetoric and Irony: Western Literacy and Western Lies* (Oxford).

Tanner, T. (1980): *Adultery in the Novel* (Baltimore).

Tatum, J. ed. (1994): *The Search for the Ancient Novel* (Baltimore).

Thalmann, W. (1988): 'Thersites: Comedy, Scapegoats, and Heroic Ideology in the *Iliad*', *TAPA* 118, 1–28.

Thomas, R. (1989): *Oral Tradition and Written Record in Classical Athens* (Cambridge).

—— (2000): *Herodotus in Context: Ethnography, Science, and the Art of Persuasion* (Cambridge).

Todd, S. (1993): *The Shape of Athenian Law* (Oxford).

—— (1996): *Lysias* (Austin).

Too, Y. L. (1995): *The Rhetoric of Identity in Isocrates: Text, Power, Pedagogy* (Cambridge).

Too, Y.L. and Livingstone, N. edd. (1998): *Pedagogy and Power: Rhetorics of Classical Learning* (Cambridge).

Vander Waerdt, P. ed. (1994): *The Socratic Movement* (Ithaca).

Vasunia, P. (2001): *The Gift of the Nile* (Berkeley).

Vernant, J-P. (1982) *The Origins of Greek Thought*, trans. J. Lloyd (London).

—— (1983): *Myth and Thought among the Greeks*, trans, J. Lloyd (London).

—— (1991): *Mortals and Immortals*, ed. F. Zeitlin (Princeton).

Vidal-Naquet, P. (1981): 'Slavery and the Rule of Women in Tradition, —— Myth and Utopia', in Gordon ed. (1981).

Vlastos, G. (1991): *Socrates: Ironist and Moral Philosopher* (Cambridge).

—— (1994): *Socratic Studies* (Cambridge).

von Reden, S. and Goldhill, S. (1999): 'Plato and the Performance of Dialogue', in Goldhill and Osborne edd. (1999).

Walsh, G. (1984): *The Varieties of Enchantment* (Chapel Hill).

Wardy, R. (1996): *The Birth of Rhetoric: Gorgias, Plato and Their Successors* (London).

Waters, K. (1985): *Herodotus the Historian* (Norman, Oklahoma).

Weiss, R. (1998): *Socrates Dissatisfied: an Analysis of Plato's Crito* (Oxford).

—— (2001): *Virtue in the Cave: Moral Enquiry in Plato's Meno* (New York).

Winkler, J. (1990): *The Constraints of Desire* (New York).

Winkler, J. and Zeitlin, F. edd. (1990): *Nothing to Do with Dionysus?* (Princeton).

Yunis, H. (1996): *Taming Democracy: Models of Political Rhetoric in Classical Athens* (Ithaca, N.Y.).

Zanker, P. (1995): *The Mask of Socrates: the Image of the Intellectual in Antiquity*, trans. A. Shapiro (Berkeley).

ABOUT THE AUTHOR

Simon Goldhill is Reader in Greek Literature and Culture at Cambridge University, and a Fellow of King's College, where he is Director of Studies in Classics. He has published widely on many aspects of Greek literature and culture including *Reading Greek Tragedy* (Cambridge, 1986), *The Poet's Voice* (Cambridge, 1991), *Aeschylus: The Oresteia* (Landmarks in World Literature) (Cambridge, 1992), and *Foucault's Virginity* (Cambridge, 1995). He has lectured all over the world, and has given many school talks in Britain, not least while acting as Schools Liaison Officer for the Cambridge Classics Faculty. He is particularly interested in literary criticism and in how Greek literature relates to the society in which it was produced.

INDEX